GUIDE TO COVERAGE OF COMMUNITIES OF WRITERS AND READERS

If you go to college, hold a job, and join a civic group, you're participating right now in the broad **academic, work,** and **public communities.**

ACADEMIC COMMUNITY	WORK COMMUNITY	PUBLIC COMMUNITY
Students, teachers, and others create and exchange knowledge through research, analysis, and interpretation.	Co-workers, managers, clients, and others exchange information, solve problems, and promote an organization.	Residents, leaders, volunteers, and others support a cause, supply information, or partici- pate in civic exchanges.

As you talk, read, and write in a community, you'll learn to recognize dif- ferent community expectations—what readers want or need—and to tailor your choices as a writer to meet those expectations.

STRATEGIES FOR WRITING AND READING IN COMMUNITIES

Throughout this book, we offer advice and techniques for addressing and participating in various communities of writers and readers. See especially the following charts, boxes, and strategies.

Understanding your writing situation (**1a**)
Designing an appropriate thesis (**2b**)
Evaluating support (**3c**)
Recognizing and adjusting to a community's style (**5a–b**)
Designing documents for readers (**6**)
Constructing an argument (**7**)
Recognizing research communities (**8a**)
Documenting sources for your audience (**12a**)
First, second, and third person in three communities (**25a**)
Recognizing and editing language varieties (**29a**)

THE
Longman Pocket Writer's Companion

SECOND EDITION

CHRIS M.
ANSON
North Carolina
State University

ROBERT A.
SCHWEGLER
University of
Rhode Island

MARCIA F.
MUTH
University of
Colorado at Denver

New York Boston San Francisco
London Toronto Sydney Tokyo Singapore Madrid
Mexico City Munich Paris Cape Town Hong Kong Montreal

Senior Acquisitions Editor: Lynn M. Huddon
Executive Marketing Manager: Megan Galvin-Fak
Managing Editor: Bob Ginsberg
Project Coordination, Text Design, and Electronic Page Makeup:
    Nesbitt Graphics, Inc.
Cover Design Manager: John Callahan
Cover Designer: Kay Petronio
Manufacturing Manager: Mary Fischer
Manufacturing Buyer: Lucy Hebard
Printer and Binder: RR Donnelley & Sons Company/Crawfordsville
Cover Printer: Coral Graphic Services, Inc.

For permission to use copyrighted material, grateful acknowledgment is made to the copyright holders on pp. vi and 251, which are hereby made part of this copyright page.

Library of Congress Cataloging-in-Publication Data

Anson, Christopher M., [date]-
    The Longman pocket writer's companion / Chris M. Anson, Robert A.
Schwegler, Marcia F. Muth.—2nd ed.
        p. cm.
    Includes index.
    ISBN 0-321-28826-2
    1. English language—Rhetoric—Handbooks, manuals, etc. 2. Report writing—
Handbooks, manuals, etc. I. Title: Pocket writer's companion. II. Schwegler, Robert A.
III. Muth, Marcia F. IV. Title.
PE1408.L67 2006
808'.042—dc22   2005001795

Copyright © 2006 by Pearson Education, Inc.

Please visit our website at http://www.ablongman.com

ISBN 0-321-28826-2

1 2 3 4 5 6 7 8 9 10—DOC—08 07 06 05

Guide for Using This Handbook

When you're a busy writer in academic, work, and public communities, you want to make the most of your time. This book is designed to help you find what you need quickly and efficiently.

Strategy 1: Try the index at the end of the book. It includes key terms, subtopics, and related entries.

Strategy 2: Use the menu inside the front cover. This menu identifies sections and chapters so you can easily find main topics.

Strategy 3: Use the table of contents inside the back cover. Skim the contents to track down the chapter or topic you need. The chapter numbers and section letters noted there are used in cross-references and are easy to spot on the tabs on each page.

Strategy 4: Match editing symbols on your paper with corresponding sections of the text. Page 265 lists common revising and editing symbols. Identify the marks on your paper, and turn to the relevant section of the text.

Strategy 5: Refer to Grammar at a Glance and the Glossary. Check pages 223–232 for useful grammar charts, or look up terms and usage questions in the Glossary beginning on page 233.

Strategy 6: Use the special features of the text.
- **Look for the "read, recognize, and revise" approach.** Many chapters, especially those on grammar and usage, first introduce a problem using a Reader's Reaction and sample sentences. Then the chapter shows how to recognize and revise or edit the problem in your writing

- **Use Read, Recognize, and Revise Ten Serious Errors.** Find this guide
SERIOUS ERROR ②   inside the back cover. Look for a sentence like yours, and turn to the section noted for advice about how to recognize and remedy the problem. Look for an icon like the one shown in the margin on the left to help you easily identify each section that discusses a serious error.
- **Apply the Strategies.** Each Strategy suggests how to apply general advice, recognize problems, or revise and edit your own writing.
- **Compare the examples with your own sentences.** Skim the draft sentences in the section that seems the most likely place to look for a problem. Find a sentence like your own. Read the explanation with it, and note any label so that you can learn how to recognize the problem. Use the revised or edited sentence as a pattern for your own changes.
- **Look for boldfaced terms.** These key terms are explained right in the text.
- **Find the ESL Advice.** If you are not a native speaker of English, use the Guide to ESL Advice (p. 264). Look for the ESL Advice integrated in the text and for reference materials in the Grammar at a Glance section (pp. 223–232).
- **Look for charts and boxes.** They make information easy to spot.
- **Turn to sample documents.** Selections from two sample research papers (13c and 14c using the MLA and APA styles) show how other students have presented their papers. Sample documents in 6e also show how you might design a paper, résumé, or newsletter.

Credits

Page 1: From ABOUT THIS LIFE by Barry Lopez, published by Knopf in 1998. **Page 12:** Copyright © 1998 from ZEN & THE ART OF STAND-UP COMEDY by Jay Sankey. Reproduced by permission of Routledge/Taylor & Francis Books, Inc. **Page 23:** The Daily Moose Newsletter. Reprinted by permission. **Page 31:** Copyright 1942 by Zora Neale Hurston; renewed © 1970 by John C. Hurston. Reprinted by permission of HarperCollins Publishers Inc. **Page 46:** Leo Reisberg, "Colleges Step Up Efforts to Combat Alcohol Abuse," THE CHRONICLE OF HIGHER EDUCATION, June 12, 1998, Vol. 44, No. 40. **Page 48:** Larry A. Tucker, "Effect of Weight Training on Self-Concept: A Profile of Those Influenced Most," RESEARCH QUARTERLY FOR EXERCISE AND SPORT, 1983. **Page 50–53:** Paula Mathieu and Ken McAllister, CRITT Web Site (Critical Resources in Teaching with Technology), 1997. http://www.engl.uic.edu/~stp/. **Page 51:** "Why Milk" Web page. Courtesy of Southeast Dairy Association. **Page 52:** "Why Does Milk Bother Me?" From National Digestive Diseases Information Clearinghouse, National Institutes of Health, (Credits continue on p. 251)

PART

1

Writing and Reading

Voices
from the Community

"Every story is an act of trust between a writer and a reader; each story, in the end, is social. Whatever a writer sets down can harm or help the community of which he or she is a part."
—Barry Lopez, "A Voice," *About This Life: Journeys on the Threshold of Memory*

1 | Writing and Reading in Communities

Writing grows from the relationship between writers and readers. Whether you are drafting a history paper, a memo at work, or a neighborhood flyer, try to envision the **community of readers and writers** you are addressing—people with shared, though not necessarily identical, interests, goals, and preferences. Their expectations help you decide how best to shape ideas, information, and experiences you want to share with them.

Participating in academic, work, and public communities means talking, reading, and especially writing. As you communicate in these broad communities, you'll find that they share some preferences—such as favoring clear, specific writing—and differ on others, such as addressing the reader as *you*. Understanding such preferences can help you recognize readers' expectations and likely responses as well as writers' opportunities and choices.

1a Understanding your writing situation

Begin by "reading" your situation, often a specific task, occasion, project, or assignment.

- What is your purpose? What do you want or need to achieve?
- How will you relate to readers? What will they expect?
- What is your subject? What do you know, or need to know, about it?

> **STRATEGY** Pinpoint your writing task.
>
> Look over your task or assignment. Draw a straight line under words (usually nouns) that specify a **topic.** Put a wavy line under action words (verbs) that tell what your writing needs to *do*, its **purpose.**
>
> **Assignment:** Analyze a magazine ad for hidden cultural assumptions. Describe what happens in the ad, noting camera angle, color, and focus.

THREE COMMUNITIES OF READERS AND WRITERS			
	ACADEMIC	**WORK**	**PUBLIC**
GOALS	Create or exchange knowledge	Solve problems, inform, promote	Persuade, participate, inform
FORMS	Analysis, interpretation, lab report, proposal, article, bibliography	Memo, letter, ad, report, minutes, proposal, instructions	Letter, flyer, newsletter, position, paper, fact sheet
WRITING CHARACTERISTICS	Reasoning, analysis, insights, evidence, detail, fair exploration	Clarity, accuracy, conciseness, focus on problem	Advocacy, evidence, shared values, recognition of others

Whatever your task and whatever your broad community (academic, work, or public), you need to address your specific readers, actual or potential. Always ask, "Exactly what do my readers expect?"

STRATEGY   Analyze your readers.

Who? How large is your audience? How well do you know them? Are they close or distant?

Expectations? Which expectations of readers are typical of the community in which you are writing?

Knowledge? What are your readers likely to know about your topic? What do they want or need to know?

Background? What defines your readers socially, culturally, or educationally? How do they think?

Relationships? Are your readers peers or superiors? What do they expect you to do? What do you expect them to do?

1b Moving from reading to writing

Good writing is often inspired by what others have written. Critical reading techniques will help you understand a text and respond to it by developing your own ideas and insights.

Reading critically. **Critical reading** begins with understanding that leads to analysis and interpretation. Before you begin reading, review the table of contents, abstract, or headings. Scan the text for key ideas and concepts. Note any background information about the author, the intended audience, or the occasion for which the text was written.

As you read, draw on the following techniques.

- Skim each section after you have read it, reviewing major points and their connections.
- Take note of what you have learned and what you find puzzling or confusing. Reread at a later time to clarify your understanding.
- Try to sum up or restate the text's main points or ideas in your own words.
- List the major insights, opinions, or ideas.

During and after reading, interact with a text in ways that help you develop your own insights and ideas.

> **STRATEGY** **Interact with a text.**
>
> - **Question.** What do you want or need to know?
> - **Synthesize.** How does the text relate to other views? What other views does it acknowledge (or fail to anticipate)?
> - **Interpret.** What does the writer mean or imply? What do you conclude about the text's outlook or bias?
> - **Assess.** How do you evaluate its value and accuracy? How does it compare to other texts being read in the community?

Turning reading into writing. Try putting your responses to a text into informal kinds of writing that you can later develop into essays or reports. Some techniques include the following.

- **Marginal comments.** In the margins of a text (if it belongs to you) or on a photocopy, write your interpretations, questions, objections, evaluations, or applications (to a class, service learning project, civic activity, or work task).
- **Journal entries.** In a journal or on note cards, respond to your reading, noting what you think or where you agree or disagree with the author.

1c Paying attention to the writing process

Experienced writers know that paying attention to all parts of the writing process generally leads to more effective writing.

Discovering and planning. To identify and develop a promising topic, use techniques such as these.

- **Freewrite** quickly by hand or at the computer for five or ten minutes. Don't stop; just slip into engaging ideas.
- Try **focused freewriting**, exploring a specific idea.
- Ask **strategic questions** to stir memories and suggest what to gather. Begin with *what, why,* and *why not.* Next try *who, where, when, how.*
- Use **interactive prompts** from the Web, computer lab, tutoring center, or your software.

To focus and organize your writing, try the following strategies. They can help you create a design or structure to guide your drafting.

- Try **clustering.** Write an idea at the center of a page, and jot down random associations. Circle key ideas; add lines to connect them.
- **List ideas and details** you want to discuss.
- **Chunk** related points and material in computer files (organized by topic or by section of the paper).
- Consider a **formal outline** (numbered and lettered sections) or a **working outline** (introduction, body, conclusion) to order points.

Drafting. Begin drafting once you have a main idea (or **thesis,** see 2a) and a general structure. Draft quickly; don't worry about perfect sentences. Or try **semidrafting**, writing until you stall out, noting *etc.* or a list instead of full text, and moving on to the next point.

Revising, editing, proofreading. Revision means critically *reading* and *reworking*. It precedes **editing** to fine-tune sentences or **proofreading** to check for small errors.

REVISING, EDITING, AND PROOFREADING

Major revision. Redraft passages, reorganize, add, and delete.

Minor revision. Adopt a reader's point of view. Rework illogical, wordy, or weak passages.

Collaborative revision. Ask peers to suggest improvements.

Editing. Improve clarity, style, and economy; check grammar, sentence structure, wording, punctuation, and mechanics.

Proofreading. Focus on details and final appearance, especially spelling, punctuation, and typing errors.

2 | Developing a Thesis

Most writing needs a clear **thesis**—a main idea, insight, or opinion that you wish to share. Announcing it in a **thesis statement** helps readers follow your reasoning and helps you organize and maintain focus.

2a Creating a thesis statement

You may choose to state your thesis near the beginning to guide readers, perhaps after introducing your topic and giving any needed background. Begin with a **rough thesis**, a sentence (or two) that identifies your perspective and states your assertion, conclusion, or opinion.

VAGUE TOPIC   Ritalin

STILL A TOPIC   The use of Ritalin for kids

STILL A TOPIC (NO ASSERTION)	Problems of Ritalin for kids with attention-deficit disorder (ADD)

READER'S REACTION: **But what should parents do?**

ROUGH THESIS (ASSERTION)	Parents should be careful about Ritalin for kids with ADD.

Extend a rough thesis, making it more precise and complex. For example, what stance should parents take: Avoid Ritalin? Use it cautiously?

EXTENDED THESIS	Although Ritalin is widely used to treat children with ADD, parents should not rely too heavily on such drugs until they have explored both their child's problem and all treatment options.

STRATEGY Sharpen your thesis until your final draft.

Treat your thesis as tentative. Refine it to offer a clear assertion—focused, limited, and yet complex enough to warrant readers' attention.

2b Designing an appropriate thesis

Refine your thesis to suit your purpose or readers.

General thesis. Readers will expect to discover your conclusions or special perspectives.

> Sooner or later, teenagers stop listening to parents and turn to each other for advice, sometimes with disastrous results.

Informative thesis. Readers will expect to learn why this information is of interest and how you'll organize it.

> When students search for online advice about financial aid, they can find help on three very different kinds of Web sites.

Argumentative thesis. Readers will expect your opinion, perhaps with other views on the issue, too.

Although bioengineered crops may pose some dangers, their potential for combating worldwide hunger justifies their careful use.

Academic thesis. Readers will expect you to state your specific conclusion and a plan to support it in terms that fit the field.

My survey of wedding announcements in local newspapers from 1960 to 2000 indicates that religious background and ethnicity have decreased in importance as factors in mate selection.

3 | Providing Support and Reasoning Clearly

Whether exploring an academic topic, making a recommendation at work, or urging people to take a stand on an issue, the path your thinking takes is called a **chain of reasoning.** Readers will find your writing logical and convincing if it's careful and critical, providing details and support suitable for your subject, purpose, and community.

3a Reasoning critically

What processes support critical reasoning?

- Exploring a question, problem, or experience
- Uniting ideas and information to reach a conclusion
- Focusing on the end point of the chain of reasoning—the main conclusion—often your thesis statement

TYPES OF CONCLUSIONS YOU MIGHT DRAW

Interpretations of meaning (experience, literature, film), importance (current event, history), or causes and effects (problem, event)

Analyses of elements (problem, situation, phenomenon, subject)

Propositions about an issue, problem, or policy

Judgments about "rightness" or "wrongness" (action, policy), quality (performance, creative work), or effectiveness (solution, course of action)

Recommendations for guidelines, policies, or responses

Warnings about consequences of action or inaction

CRITICAL REASONING IN THREE MAJOR COMMUNITIES			
	ACADEMIC	**WORK**	**PUBLIC**
GOAL	Analysis of text, phenomenon, or creative work to interpret, explain, or offer insights	Analysis of problems to supply information and propose solutions	Participation in democratic processes to contribute, inform, or persuade
REASONING PROCESS	Detailed reasoning leading to specific conclusions	Accurate analysis of problem or need with clear explanation of solution	Plausible reasoning to support own point of view without ranting
EVIDENCE	Specific references to detailed evidence, with citations of others' work	Sufficient evidence to show the problem's importance and justify a solution	Relevant evidence, often local, to substantiate views and probabilities
EXAMPLE	Present and support new explanation of Alzheimer's	Describe marketing strategy for Alzheimer's drug	Propose new community facility for Alzheimer's patients

> **STRATEGY** **Focus on your conclusions.**
>
> List all your conclusions, interpretations, or opinions. What others come to mind? Which are main and which secondary? What explanation or evidence connects these points? Does each lead logically to the next?

3b Providing support

A convincing chain of reasoning gives readers information that supports generalizations. **Information** includes facts of all kinds—examples, data, details, quotations—that you present as reliable, confirmable, or generally undisputed. **Generalizations** are conclusions based on and supported by information. Information turns into **evidence** when it's used to persuade a reader that an idea is reasonable.

TYPES OF EVIDENCE

Examples of an event, idea, person, or place, brief or extended, from personal experience or research

Details of an idea, place, situation, or phenomenon

Information about times, places, participants, numbers, consequences, surroundings, and relationships

Statistics, perhaps presented in tables or charts

Background on context, history, or effects

Quotations from experts, participants, or other writers

3c Evaluating support

Assess evidence critically. How **abundant** is it? Is it **sufficient** to support conclusions? Is it **relevant, accurate,** and **well documented?**

STRATEGY **Align your evidence with your thesis.**

> **General thesis.** Supply evidence that fits your claim and readers' expectations: statistics, interviews, examples from experience.
>
> **Informative thesis.** Give evidence showing a subject's elements.
>
> **Argumentative thesis.** Supply information, examples, and quotations to support your stand, answer objections, and refute opposing views.
>
> **Academic thesis.** Provide evidence that meets the discipline's standards; cite contributions of others.

4 | Paragraphing for Readers

Every time you indent to begin a new paragraph, you signal academic, workplace, or public readers to watch for a shift in topic or emphasis.

4a Focusing paragraphs

A **focused paragraph** has a clear topic and main idea that guide readers through the specifics of your discussion.

STRATEGY **Check your paragraph focus.**

- What is your main point in this paragraph?
- How many different ideas does it cover?
- Does it elaborate on the main idea? Do details fit?
- Have you announced your focus to readers? Where?

Help readers recognize a paragraph's focus by stating your topic and main idea or perspective in a **topic sentence.** Place this sentence at a paragraph's end, leave it unstated but clearly implied, or add a clarifying sentence to explain further. When you want readers to grasp the point right away, put this sentence first.

> When writing jokes, it's a good idea to avoid vague generalizations. Don't just talk about "fruit" when you can talk about "an apple." Strong writing creates a single image for everyone in the crowd, each person imagining a very similar thing. But when you say "fruit," people are either imagining several different kinds of fruit or they aren't really thinking of anything in particular, and both things can significantly reduce their emotional investment in the joke. But when you say "an apple," everyone has *a clear picture,* and thus a feeling.
>
> —Jay Sankey, "Zen and the Art of Stand-Up Comedy"

4b Making paragraphs coherent

A paragraph is **coherent** if each sentence leads clearly to the next, forming an easy-to-understand arrangement. When sentences are out of logical order or jump abruptly, readers may struggle to follow the thought.

STRATEGY Check your paragraph coherence.

- Does the paragraph repeat key words and synonyms naming the topic and main points? Do these words begin or end sentences, or are they buried in the middle?
- What transition words relate sentences?
- What parallel structures emphasize similar ideas? (See 26a–b.)
- Are ideas and details arranged logically?

Place key words to keep readers aware of the arrangement of ideas.

> **People married for a long time** often develop similar **facial features. Younger couples** display only chance resemblances between their **faces.** Because **they** share emotions for many years, however, **older couples** acquire similar **expressions.**

USEFUL TRANSITIONS FOR SHOWING RELATIONSHIPS

Time and sequence: next, later, after, meanwhile, while, immediately, earlier, first, second, third, shortly, in the future, subsequently, soon, since, finally, last, as long as, at that time

Comparison: likewise, similarly, also, again, in comparison

Contrast: in contrast, on the one hand . . . on the other hand, however, although, yet, but, nevertheless, at the same time, regardless

Examples: for example, for instance, such as, thus, namely, specifically, to illustrate

Cause and effect: as a result, consequently, due to, for this reason, accordingly, if . . . then, as a consequence

Place: next to, above, behind, beyond, between, here, there, opposite, to the right, in the background, over, under

Addition: and, too, moreover, in addition, besides, next, also, finally

Concession: of course, naturally, granted, it is true that, certainly

Conclusion: in conclusion, as a result, as the data show

Repetition: in other words, once again, to repeat

Summary: on the whole, to sum up, in short, therefore

4c Developing paragraphs

Paragraph development provides the informative examples, facts, details, explanations, or arguments readers expect to support a conclusion.

UNDERDEVELOPED

Recycling is always a good idea—or almost always. Recycling some products, even paper, may require more energy from fossil fuels and more valuable natural resources than making them the first time.

READER'S REACTION: I need to know more before I agree. Which products? How much energy does recycling take? What resources are consumed?

STRATEGY   Check your paragraph development.

Highlight the material that develops your paragraph. Do you present enough to *inform* readers? Do you adequately *support* generalizations?

Patterns for development help you accomplish tasks in ways that readers will easily recognize.

PATTERNS FOR PARAGRAPH DEVELOPMENT

Narrating: tell a story or anecdote; recreate events

Describing: provide detail about a scene, object, character, or feeling

Comparing and contrasting: explore similarities or differences; evaluate alternatives

Explaining a process: provide directions; explain how a mechanism, procedure, or natural process operates

Dividing: separate into parts; explore their relationships

Classifying: sort into groups; explain their relationships

Defining: explain a term; illustrate a concept

Analyzing causes and effects: consider why something did or might happen

---

5 | Matching Style and Strategy to a Community of Readers

Should you use *I* or *we*—or *you*? Should you add technical terms? Such choices depend less on your "voice" than on **community style**—preferences taken for granted by communities of readers and writers. Likewise, the goals and strategies you choose should reflect an understanding of the community of writers and readers you are addressing.

5a   Recognizing a community's style

Consider the following to help you understand your options as a writer.

Formality. Do readers expect writing that is formal, complicated, and technical or relaxed and direct?

Writer's stance. How do writers identify themselves, readers, and the topic: *I, we, you, he, she, it, they*?

Language. What **diction**—word choices—do readers favor: vivid or neutral phrases, logical or informal links, technical or everyday terms?

STYLE IN THREE MAJOR COMMUNITIES			
	ACADEMIC	**WORK**	**PUBLIC**
FORMALITY	Formality supports analytical approach and values of the field	Informality reflects or builds teamwork or closeness	Informality reveals personal involvement with serious issues
WRITER'S STANCE	Observer (*he, she, it*) or participant (*I, we*)	Team member (*we*) with personal concern (*I, you*)	Involved person (*I, you*) or representative (*we, you*)
LANGUAGE	Technical terms and methods of the field	Plain or technical terms but little vivid, figurative wording	Lively and emotional; few technical terms and little slang
DISTANCE	Objective and dispassionate, not personal or emotional	Supportive, committed closeness with mutual respect	Passionate and personal about cause, issue, or group
EXAMPLE	Presentation of data and findings from experiment	Instructions for new marketing campaign	Pamphlet encouraging people to join recycling program

Distance. Is a writer typically distant or involved, an insider or outsider, a participant or observer?

5b Adjusting to a community's style

Examine your community's style as you read typical documents. For example, academic writers tend to rely on formal analysis using a discipline's terms and methods. Often distant observers, they may use *I*, depending on the field, but seldom address readers directly. In contrast, work communities share values such as efficiency and service, often using *we* to build teamwork. In public exchanges, writers may be dedicated partisans, speaking individually (*I*) or collectively (*we*).

5c Recognizing a community's expectations

The strategies you employ in your writing should take into account your audience's expectations. The following tips may help you understand the ways readers approach your work and the ways you can address their expectations.

What academic readers expect. In general, academic readers will ask you to do the following.

- Analyze or interpret a text or an event.
- Review and cite related theory and research.
- Reason logically and critically about a question.
- Bring fresh insights, and draw your own conclusions.

> **STRATEGY** Tips for academic writing.
> - State your thesis and main points clearly.
> - Use pertinent detail to support your views.
> - Write clearly and logically, even on a complex topic.
> - Acknowledge other views as you explore a topic.

What workplace readers expect. Workplace readers will expect your writing to accomplish objectives such as these.

- Provide or request information
- Analyze problems
- Recommend actions or solutions
- Identify and evaluate alternatives

STRATEGY **Tips for workplace writing.**

- Focus on the task, problem, or goal.
- Present the issue clearly and accurately.
- Organize efficiently, and summarize for busy readers.
- Use concise, clear, direct prose.

What public readers expect. Members of an organization, possible supporters of a cause, public officials, community activists, local residents, and other public audiences will look to you to do the following.

- Provide issue-oriented information, especially local background, data, and evidence.
- Encourage civic involvement and decision making.
- Persuade others to support a cause or issue.

STRATEGY **Tips for public writing.**

- Persuade, enlighten, alert, or energize readers to act.
- Recommend policies, actions, or solutions.
- Be an advocate for your cause.
- Present relevant evidence to support your position.
- Recognize the interests and goals of others.

6 | Designing Documents for Readers

What makes your research report, essay, or letter memorable—clear, persuasive, and easy to read? The answer often lies in document design, considering the look of the page or screen and the processes of readers.

6a Planning your document

To design effective documents, sketch sample pages containing design features or prepare a list of specifications that answers these questions.

- What kind of format or document do my readers expect?
- How will I lay out the pages?
- How will I highlight the organization? Will I provide a table of contents? Will I use color?
- What font, typeface, and type size will I use?
- Will I integrate visual aids? Which ones?
- What are the copyright or legal issues when using others' materials?

6b Laying out your document

Layout is the arrangement of words, sentences, lists, tables, graphs, and pictures on a printed page or screen. Supply visual cues for readers, but don't overwhelm your text.

> **STRATEGY** Highlight to direct the reader's eye.
>
> - Use **boldface,** *italics,* shading, rules, and boxes to signal distinctions, to connect, and to divide.
> - Set off items in lists with numbers, letters, or bullets.

- Use CAPITALS, exclamation points (!!), and other cues sparingly for emphasis. Limit underlining (especially in Web pages with links).
- Use color to meet goals (such as warning), prioritize, trace a theme or sequence, or code symbols.
- Leave **white space**—open space not filled by other design elements— to break dense text into chunks.

Headings are phrases that forecast content or structure. Often larger and darker, they catch a reader's eye and lead to information.

STRATEGY   Design useful headings.

- Orient headings to your task or readers: **Deducting Student Loan Interest,** not **Student Loans.**
- Position headings uniformly (for example, center one level but begin another at the left margin).
- Add white space between headings and text.
- Define heading levels consistently with visual features (font, style, position such as left margin or centered).
- Keep the wording of each level of heading parallel whenever possible.

6c Using type features

Consider readers' expectations as you judiciously use software options.

Type size and weight. Both 10- and 12-point type are easy to read; the latter is most common in academic papers. Save sizes above 12 points for special purposes (visuals, flyers, posters). Type weight (letter width and stroke thickness) can also be used to highlight.

8 point   10 point   12 point   16 point

Typefaces. Serif fonts have "little feet" or small strokes at the end of each letterform. Sans serif fonts lack them.

N   Serif   N   Sans serif

Readers tend to find serif type easier to read in text while sans serif works well in titles, headings, labels, and material onscreen. Reserve decorative fonts for brochures, invitations, or posters.

6d Using visuals

Drawings, diagrams, and photographs can speed communication. **Tables** order text or numbers in columns and rows. **Graphs** rely on two labeled axes (vertical and horizontal), using lines or bars to relate variables. **Pie charts** show percentages of a whole.

STRATEGY   Integrate visuals with text.

- Choose simple visual aids that make a point; avoid decorative filler.
- Place a visual near related text; connect it verbally.
- Label all graphics as figures (except for tables), number them, and supply short, accurate captions. (See 12c.)
- Credit sources for all borrowed graphics, and respect copyright.

6e Sample documents

The following samples show document design in action.

Sample Academic Paper with Illustration, MLA Format

↑ 1 inch

↑ 1/2 inch
Garcia 1

Daisy Garcia
Professor L. Miles
HPR 101
17 December 2003

Rebuilding

1 inch →

September 11, 2001, marks a day when your
feelings of shock and loss of direction matched with
others across the country no matter where you were or what
you were doing when the twin towers of the World Trade
Center collapsed. The various proposals for building on
the site have been ambitious, breathtaking, moving, and,
above all, quite different in perspective and style. . . .

Freedom Tower is designed to stand as the tallest
building in the world in its completion at a symbolic
height as a 1,776-foot spire. The antenna structure will be
the home of various channels in the NY area and have a
representational design relating
to the statue of liberty. David
M. Childs is collaborating with
Libeskind as the design
architect. It will contain a
vertical garden known as
"Gardens of the World,"
observation decks, and programs
for recreational commercial use.
The commercial buildings are
going to be designed by the
other three architects chosen by
Silverstein. There are about 10
million square feet of office
space in five towers and 880,000
square feet of retail space. The
Wedge of Light is an area designed and aligned with the
heavens so that on September 11th of each year, it is lit.

Fig. 1. Daniel Libeskind
and David M. Childs,
Freedom Tower design

1. Title centered with no extra space
   before or after
2. Integrates illustration next to discussion
   in text
3. Supplies figure number with label that
   properly credits the artist, and identifies
   work's title and location or source

Sample Workplace Résumé

Tammy Jo Helton
550 Sundown Ct., Dayton, OH 45420
453-555-5555   TJ@mailnow.com

CERTIFICATION
Elementary Education (grades 1-8)
Bachelor of Arts, August 2004, Wright State University, Dayton, OH

EDUCATION
Wright State University, 2001-2004, College of Education
Sinclair Community College, 2000-2001, general education
Wayne High School, 2000 graduate, college preparatory

AWARDS
Phi Kappa Phi National Honor Society 2003, 2004
Dean's list 2002, 2003, 2004

TEACHING EXPERIENCE

Student Teaching
Seventh grade physical science, L.T. Ball Junior High, Tipp City, OH
Planned and implemented lessons while maintaining classroom control.

Observation
Shilohview, Trotwood, OH
Implemented preplanned lessons.

Teaching
Sixth grade religious education class, Dayton, OH
Currently responsible for planning and implementing lessons.

WORK EXPERIENCE
Goal Line Sports Grill, 2001-present: Server, cash register, supervisor
Frisch's Big Boy, 1999-2001: Server, inventory, preparation
Shilohview Park, 1998-2000: Park Counselor, activity planner

INTERESTS AND ACTIVITIES
Took dance lessons for 10 years; played drums in the school band.

References available on request.

1. Centers name, address, phone, and email address
2. Uses capitals for main headings
3. Separates page into sections using white space
4. Uses short lines for compressed information
5. Centers closing information

Sample Newsletter, Designed by Student

Thursday
July 8th, 2003

Volume XX
Issue 2

The Daily Moose

North America's Only Newspaper Devoted to Moose Lovers Everywhere. Twenty-Two Years and Growing

Big Moose Comes From Small Dreams

Staff Reporter: Andrea White

Growing up, your favorite animal may have been a cat, dog, or turtle. Even as exotic as parrots, giraffes and elephants. But in areas north of Chicago and Boston, children wish for pets like deer, caribou and even moose. Moose usually occupy areas in the northern United States and Canada, finding them in southern California is quite unusual. However, traveling to Orange County, California you might see dozens, even hundreds of these winter-weather giants. Mainly Seconds, a craft/antique store in Orange County, has a display of numerous moose paraphernalia all collected by the "Moose" himself, Mike Bonk.

In 1982, Mike's first store opened and received a gift from his wife and former employees. It was a corduroy moose head with a plaque inscribed, "The Moose is Loose". This present hangs on the wall near the entrance next to painted words, *The Moose Museum*. The museum started when Mike put his personal items on display around the store. It seemed that as the store increased and prospered, his collection did also. Soon there was so much moose collectibles; it formed itself into a museum.

The Moose Museum Located at Mainly Seconds.

This museum is not like any other. Set in the back section of the store, it consists of about fifty cases and 10 aisles of various products either resembling or being moose associated. "If it's moose, it's in here" Mike said during a recent interview. And it's true (Cont. on page 2).

The Moose Museum
Cordially Invites You . . .

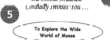

To Explore the Wide
World of Moose

Come experience the
Northern Wilderness in
Sunny California.
New Exhibits! More Moose!

789 S. Tustin Avenue   555-9876

Warning: Moose X-ing

Travel columnist: Caroline Cesserta

My family and I always agonize about where to travel for our yearly summer vacation. This year, my daughter and I agreed on a nice mountain lodge in Colorado while my husband and other daughter sided on a tropical getaway to Mexico. To compromise, we decided to tour California starting from the Mexican border up to Oregon. One of my personal favorite spots is very unusual store I discovered when we were stopped at a rest stop and someone noticed my moose decal on the back window. (Cont. Pg. 2)

1. Selects varied typefaces and sizes for a system of headings
2. Uses single page column for lead story
3. Integrates photograph and text
4. Uses double-column format for additional text
5. Encloses highlighted text in oval "box"

7 | Constructing an Argument

In argumentative writing, you present and endorse an outlook, opinion, or course of action. You persuade by focusing on reasons, evidence, and values to encourage readers to agree with your opinion or proposal.

7a Identifying an issue

At the heart of occasions calling for argumentative writing is an **issue,** that is, a topic about which you and your audience can recognize two (or more) clearly differing, worthwhile opinions. Many arguments address **existing issues,** ongoing disagreements about either broad issues (e.g., gun control or global warming) or specific concerns (e.g., a new campus drinking policy or local limits on development). To identify **potential issues,** try evaluating the consequences of a policy, questioning the "taken for granted" ("Do diesels always pollute?") or questioning widely held opinions (*Opinion:* Early decision programs benefit college applicants. *Response:* Do they really?)

	PUBLIC	WORK	ACADEMIC
GENERAL	Genetically altered foods Violence and sex on television	Child care at work Ethnically targeted marketing	Standardized testing Affirmative action in college admissions
LOCAL	A local crusade against a television series	Discipline policies at Abtech's ChildCare	Housing regulations at Nontanko River U

7b Developing an argumentative thesis

To argue effectively, you need to identify your own opinion (your **claim**) and communicate it to readers in an **argumentative thesis statement.**

Explore and clarify your perspective. Begin by articulating your opinion to yourself to focus your ideas, values, and feelings. Write informally about your intuitive reactions to your chosen issue. Does the issue make you feel scorn, pity, fear, or outrage? List the specific elements of the issue to which you respond most strongly and sum up your responses. Identify facts, examples, and ideas that support your opinions. Then think about objections to your view, and list them.

Focus and revise your claim. Limit the scope of your argument by identifying a specific claim and its purpose. Do you want to argue that an activity or belief is good or bad? If so, you are asking readers to agree with a **value judgment.** Do you want to persuade them to support a course of action? If so, you are asking them to agree with a **policy.** Do you want readers to agree with an explanation? If so, you are asking them to endorse an **interpretation.**

STRATEGY   **State and revise your claim in memos to yourself.**

Write a memo explaining the claim and your purpose for writing.

> To: Self
> From: Me
>
> I find using roadblocks to catch drunk drivers really disturbing. I know it is important to keep drunk drivers off the road, but I think this remedy is extreme. I guess I want readers to agree that roadblocks violate civil liberties and should be banned.

Revise your claim to reflect what you discover through your research. Then write yourself a second memo.

Create (and revise) a thesis statement. An explicit thesis makes your claim clear to readers and helps them follow your reasoning by

1. Identifying a specific issue and your opinion.
2. Providing a clear and logical statement of your argumentative claim.
3. Suggesting a general direction for your argument.
4. Indicating related claims or opinions.

STRATEGY   Revise your thesis statement.

- **State your thesis** in a sentence (or two), using sentence patterns like "*X* should be altered/banned/approved because . . ."; "I propose this plan/policy/action because . . ."; or "*Y* is beneficial/ineffective/harmful because . . . ."
- **Check your tentative thesis** to see whether it blurs your specific purposes for arguing or makes illogical assumptions.

    BLURRED AND   Police should stop conducting unconstitutional roadblocks
    ILLOGICAL   and substitute more frequent visual checks of erratic driving to identify people who are driving while intoxicated.

- **Revise to focus** your thesis on a clear issue, a single claim, or two related claims you will argue in appropriate order.

    SINGLE   Roadblocks used to identify drunk drivers are unconstitu-
    PROPOSITIONS   tional because they violate important civil liberties.

                         Frequent visual checks for erratic driving can effectively identify intoxicated drivers.

7c   Developing reasons and supporting evidence

To encourage readers to agree with your argumentative claim, you need to give them a series of reasons, each followed by evidence.

TENTATIVE THESIS   Coursework for certification should continue after people start teaching because this efficient approach can increase the number of dedicated new teachers.

REASON 1   People learn a skill or activity best while doing it.

EVIDENCE: **comparisons to medical internships and residencies; reports on innovative teacher training**

REASON 2   Practicing teachers are often more motivated learners than are pre-service teachers.

EVIDENCE: **information from scholarly article comparing responses of participants in pre-service and in-service courses**

REASON 3 (COUNTER-ARGUMENT)   New teachers will suceed in their first jobs, especially if their schools supervise and support them.

Varied evidence helps develop your reasons effectively by

- Providing logical justification for your opinions and reasoning.
- Encouraging readers to trust your conclusions and proposals and helping them understand your reasoning and connect it with their experiences and values.
- Helping readers envision a proposed course of action or new policy.

Examples from your own or others' experience—events, people, ideas, objects, feelings, stories, images, and texts—can support a claim and draw readers to your point of view. Quotations and ideas from authorities on a subject or issue add to the reasons for readers to agree with your point of view. Detailed information available on most issues includes statistics, technical information, results of surveys and interviews, background information, and historical detail. Visual evidence is of two kinds: (1) details, facts, and statistics in graphs, tables, or other figures, and (2) photographs or drawings that are evidence in themselves. Visuals can present complex evidence, highlight key points, and appeal to values and emotions. Coloring sections of a map red to indicate regions with severe environmental problems can make a powerful statement, for example.

7d Presenting counterarguments

Traditional argument is like debate: you imagine an adversary who doesn't go along with your ideas and then you try to undermine that adversary's points or **counterarguments.** In most contemporary arguments, you should acknowledge alternate points of view not so much to "win" as to convince others of the validity of your views.

STRATEGY   **Develop counterarguments.**

Divide a sheet of paper into three columns. On the left, list the main points supporting your opinion. Write opposing points in the middle column as if you oppose your original stance. On the right, list possible defenses to these counterarguments. Note any sources that would support your argument.

7e Reasoning logically

Effective argument assembles your opinions and supporting evidence in an order that reflects a chain of reasoning and avoids flaws in logic.

- **Reasoning from consequences.** You argue for or against an action or outlook, based on real or likely consequences, good or bad.
- **Reasoning from comparisons.** You argue for or against a policy or point of view based on similar situations, problems, or actions.
- **Reasoning from authority and testimony.** You draw evidence from recognized experts or from people with relevant experience.
- **Reasoning from examples and statistics.** You draw on events, situations, and problems presented as illustrations or as statistics.

Data-warrant-claim reasoning. This form of reasoning, proposed by philosopher Stephen Toulmin, identifies several kinds of statements reasonable people make when they argue: *data* correspond to your evidence, *claim* to your conclusion, and *warrant* to the mental process by which a reader connects the data to the claim. It answers the question "How?"

Suppose you are examining the relative safety of cars. As data, you have a study on the odds of injury in different models of cars. To argue effectively, you need to show readers *how* the data and your claim are connected, what patterns (probable facts—warrants) link the data to your claim.

DATA

Ratings of each car model by likelihood of injury (scale: 1–10)

CLAIM

For the average consumer, buying a large car is a good way to reduce the likelihood of being injured in an accident.

WARRANT

- The cars in the ratings fall into three easily recognized groups: small, medium, large. (probable fact)
- The large cars as a group have a lower average likelihood of injury to passengers than either of the other groups. (probable fact)
- Although some other cars have low likelihood of injury, almost all the large cars seem safe. (assertion + probable fact)
- Few consumers will go over the crash ratings to see which models get good or poor scores. (assertion)

Logical and emotional appeals. Logical and emotional appeals can enhance your credibility as a writer if you take the time to consider your readers and arrange your reasons and evidence in ways that most people will accept as reasonable and convincing. Emotional strategies focus on the values, beliefs, and emotions that can engage readers and motivate them to care about an issue. However, such appeals are generally best accepted when they are also supported by logical strategies—reasoning based on likely good or bad consequences, relevant comparisons, authoritative experts, trustworthy testimony, pertinent illustrations, and statistics. Watch for logical fallacies or flaws in reasoning as you evaluate your evidence and shape your argument.

A **logical fallacy** is a flaw in reasoning that undermines your argument. Logical fallacies take some common forms.

- **Faulty Cause-Effect Relationship** (*post hoc, ergo propter hoc* reasoning—"after this, therefore because of this"): attempts to persuade you that because one event follows another, the first causes the second.

  The increase in violence on television is making the crime rate soar.

READER'S REACTION: **This *may* be true, but no evidence here links the two situations.**

- **False Analogy:** compares two things that seem, but aren't, comparable.

  Raising the speed limit is like offering free cocktails at a meeting of recovering alcoholics.

  READER'S REACTION: **I don't see the connection. Most drivers aren't recovering from an addiction to high-speed driving.**

- **Red Herring:** distracts readers from the real argument.

  Gun control laws need to be passed as soon as possible to decrease domestic violence and accidents. The people who think guns should not be controlled are probably criminals themselves.

  READER'S REACTION: **The second sentence doesn't follow logically or add support. It's just a distracting attack on people who disagree.**

- **Ad Hominem:** attacks the person, not the issue.

  Of course Walt Smith would support a bill to aid farmers—he owns several farms in the Midwest.

  READER'S REACTION: **I'd like to hear reactions to his ideas, please.**

- **Begging the Question:** presents assumptions as facts.

  Most people try to be physically fit; obviously, they fear getting old.

  READER'S REACTION: **I don't see any evidence that people fear aging—or that they are working on their physical fitness, either.**

- **Circular Reasoning:** supports an assertion with the assertion itself.

  The university should increase funding of intramural sports because it has a responsibility to back its sports programs financially.

  READER'S REACTION: **So the university should fund sports because it should fund sports?**

Voices
from the Community

"Research is formalized curiosity. It is poking and prying with a purpose." —Zora Neale Hurston, *Dust Tracks on a Road*

8 | Planning and Conducting Research

You may be in the library working on your psychology paper on stress, searching the Web about company-sponsored child care, or surveying neighbors on new city recreation options. Each task raises its own questions and requires different research strategies, sources, and forms for turning inquiry into writing. Each draws on its own narrow research community but addresses a broader audience—academic, work, or public.

8a Recognizing research communities

Successful research writing goes beyond simply conveying information. By blending their own insights with material from print, electronic, or field sources, researchers increase readers' understanding. Writers and readers together ideally form a **research community,** a web of people and texts that (1) share a perspective and focus—a **research topic,** (2) agree on **research questions** worth asking, and (3) use shared terms, **keywords** that form a **research thread** linking topics and resources.

8b Recognizing research topics

Your assignment may launch your inquiry. It may specify the deadlines, format, and sources expected by your teacher, supervisor, or organization.

STRATEGY **Begin your inquiry with questions.**

- What problem, issue, question, or event piques your curiosity?
- What new, contradictory, or intriguing ideas turn up as you read?
- What ideas do Web surfing, class discussion, or meetings in a work or public setting suggest?
- What would your readers also like to know?

AUDIENCE EXPECTATIONS FOR RESEARCH WRITING			
	ACADEMIC	**WORK**	**PUBLIC**
GOAL	Explain, interpret, analyze, synthesize	Document problems, propose, improve	Support policy or action
READER EXPECTATIONS	Detailed evidence, varied sources	Clear, precise, direct information	Accessible, fair persuasion
TYPICAL QUESTIONS	What does it mean? Why does it happen?	What is the problem? How can we solve it?	How can we improve a policy or situation?
TYPICAL FORMS	Paper to interpret, inform, or argue	Proposal, feasibility study, report	Speech, pamphlet, letter, fact sheet
SAMPLE RESEARCH QUESTION ON COSMETICS	What gender roles do ads reinforce?	How can we develop local packaging?	Are animal tests of cosmetics necessary?

8c Identifying keywords

Libraries, search engines, and databases use keywords to categorize and access information. As you consider research topics, note recurring words (*alcohol*), names (*John Glenn*), and phrases (*early childhood*).

STRATEGY   Identify and use keywords.

- Write down the keywords that might refer to your topic. Note synonyms (*maturation* for *growth*).
- Refine your list by adding keywords you encounter in print or electronic sources. Drop any you encounter rarely. Use this list to search library catalogs, research databases, and the Web.
- If your keywords produce too many possible sources, look for more precise terms used by people writing about your topic.
- Integrate your keywords into your research questions, thesis, and paper.

8d Developing research questions

Research questions help you focus as you filter information and lead to your **thesis,** the main idea that you explore, support, or illustrate.

Academic. What do experts ask or say about your topic? Do you agree or disagree? What can you add? What ambiguities remain?

Work. What is the problem or situation? What do you propose? Why will it work, work better, or cost less?

Public. What policy or program do you propose? Whom does it benefit? Why? What might its effects be?

Summer Arrigo-Nelson and Jennifer Figliozzi developed these research questions on student drinking for a report on a campus problem.

- Will students with permission to drink at home have different drinking behaviors at college than those without such permission?
- Do students feel that a correlation exists between drinking behaviors at home and at college?

STRATEGY State your research questions early.

- Aim for two or three direct questions, and embed your keywords.
- Pose questions without clear answers, not with an obvious consensus.
- Design questions that will matter to your audience.

8e Developing search strategies

A **search strategy** is a plan for locating resources to answer research questions and support your thesis (2a–b). It can include **library sources** (books, articles, databases, media materials), **online sources** (Web sites and discussion groups), and **field sources** (interviews, surveys, and observations).

Primary sources provide information in original (or close-to-original) form: historical and literary texts, letters, videos, survey results, and other data. **Secondary sources** explain, analyze, summarize, or interpret primary sources, telling you what others have said and what issues are debated by scholars and other writers.

STRATEGY   **Design a search strategy.**

- **List resources.** Include the kinds of resources you plan to use—books, scholarly journals, newspapers, Web sites, interviews, and surveys. Explore potential resources under the heading *What about . . . ?*
- **Identify search tools.** Pay attention to specialized research tools.
  - Indexes of magazine and newspaper articles—*InfoTrac, New York Times Index, Wall Street Journal Index*
  - Indexes of articles in scholarly journals—*Social Sciences Index, MLA International Bibliography, Education Index*
  - Academic and professional databases with built-in search engines—*EBSCOhost, LexisNexis, OCLC First Search*
  - Specialized Web search engines and indexed databases—*Highbeam, AltaVista, Cata List, Dogpile, PAIS*
- **Draw on keywords and research questions.** Use a list of keywords (see 8c) to search indexes, databases, and the Web. Use keywords and your research questions to focus and guide your search.
- **Revise.** Update your research questions, search strategy, and keywords as your research evolves.

8f   Selecting resources for a working bibliography

Build a **working bibliography** of possible sources addressing your research questions. Consult indexes, catalogs, search engines, or databases (see 9a–d, 10b).

Include

- Items whose titles suggest rich and relevant resources
- Recent and varied sources, from broad surveys to focused studies
- Sources from bibliographies with *annotations* or search engines with *abstracts* that summarize content and utility
- More sources than needed, to allow for any not available or useful

Exclude
- Sources that may be difficult to obtain or that lack credibility (see 11c–d)
- Sources with a questionable connection to your topic

8g Keeping track of your sources and notes

Select a system for recording bibliographic information and taking notes (see 11a) so you can easily document sources. Link your notes to keywords, to research questions, and to page numbers in your sources.

Note cards. If you prefer cards—easy to group or add—write each bibliography entry on a 3" × 5" and each reading note on a 4" × 6" card.

Research notebook. In a notebook you can add marginal notes, attach colored dots or flags, or duplicate pages to cut up as you organize.

Electronic notes. Software files that resemble onscreen cards easily transfer to a reference list or draft paper. Some programs will format entries using the style you select. Be sure to record the following information.

BOOKS	ARTICLES	ELECTRONIC SOURCES
Author(s), editor(s), translator(s)	Author(s)	Name of source
Title: Subtitle	Title: Subtitle	Address/URL/access route/vendor
City: publisher, date	Periodical name	Name of database
Call number and library location	Volume (& issue)	Date of publication or last revision
	Date	Date of access
	Page number(s)	Author or sponsoring group
	Library location	

8h Pulling your research materials together

Finding resources is half the challenge; managing the information that you locate is the other half.

- Gather your notes, copies, printouts, files, and other material.
- Sort your resources, and track down missing material.
- Use your research questions as guides to main points and subtopics. Use keywords, color codes, or stacks of material to sort by category.
- If a category contains little information, drop it or do more research. If it contains lots of material, decide whether to break it into subtopics.
- If you need more information, consult a librarian, instructor, or specialist in the field.

9 | Finding Library and Database Resources

Libraries give you access to books and articles (both print and electronic), online research databases, recordings, microforms, and art. Research databases are available on the Web and, increasingly, through college and university libraries.

9a Finding library resources

Visit your library—or its home page—to explore resources for almost all fields of academic, work, or public interest. Start with **ready references,** general encyclopedias, atlases, dictionaries, and statistical abstracts. Then turn to **specialized encyclopedias** and **dictionaries,** as varied as *Current Biography; Encyclopedia of Pop, Rock, and Soul;* and the *McGraw-Hill Encyclopedia of Science and Technology.* Check useful **bibliographies,** listings of resources such as the *MLA International Bibliography* on literature and language or the *International Bibliography of the Social Sciences.*

STRATEGY **Talk to information specialists.**

Reference librarians can help you refine a search strategy, improve keyword searches, and locate materials on campus or on loan.

Periodicals appear regularly with articles by many authors. **Online periodicals** may place past articles in electronic archives; other **Web sites** act like periodicals, adding material as the site is updated. Through your library, the Web, or search engines, you can access **periodical indexes,** some of which supply brief summaries (or abstracts).

Your library will offer access to **general indexes** such as *Academic Index, InfoTrac, OCLC/World Catalog, PAIS (Public Affairs, Information Services),* or *NewsBank.* Academic libraries also supply **specialized indexes** such as *BIZZ (Business Index), Government Documents Catalog Service (GDCS/GPO Index), Current Index to Journals in Education (CIJE), Social Sciences Index,* or *Biological and Agricultural Index.*

PRINT PERIODICALS			
	MAGAZINES	**JOURNALS**	**NEWSPAPERS**
READERS?	General public	Academics, professionals	General public
WRITERS?	Staff, journalists	Scholars, experts	Staff, journalists
HOW OFTEN?	Monthly, weekly	Quarterly, monthly	Daily, weekly
APPEARANCE?	Color, photos, glossy paper, sidebars	Dense text, data, plain paper, little color	Columns, headlines, photos, some color

9b Using library resources

First identify resources, then find them. Start with the library home page or **online catalog.** Search for an *author's name,* the *title* of a work or periodical, or a *keyword.* If you find several items (each listed in a **brief display**), click on one to call up its **full display.** You may also expand a search to related topics, authors, or works or follow related links (see 10c). Print or record your results, including call numbers and locations.

Government documents include general and technical reports, pamphlets, and regulations issued by Congress, federal agencies, and state or local governments. The *Monthly Catalog of U.S. Government Publications* can help direct your search, as can the *Government Information Sharing Project* <http://govinfo.kerr.orst.edu>, *Library of Congress* <http://www.loc.gov>, and *Thomas Legislative Information* site <http://thomas.loc.gov>.

Special collections house many documents, including those on local history. **Audiovisual collections** contain tapes, films, and recordings. **Microform collections** contain copies of periodicals and documents.

9c Finding research databases

Researchers (student and professional) have come to rely on electronic databases for all kinds of information, especially texts of scholarly articles and general-interest periodical articles. University and public libraries have greatly increased the available number of **online databases.** Most focus on specialized fields and are especially useful for researchers.

You can access research databases at library terminals, through a library's Web site, or through the Web site of a commercial database company such as *Highbeam* or *LexisNexis.* You can generally search a database by author, title, and keyword or by categories appropriate for the materials in a collection. Most databases are updated frequently. Consult library handouts or the information screen of a database to learn what resources it provides and the range of dates for the materials it contains.

9d Using research databases

Databases are of several kinds, varying according to the information and texts they provide.

- **Full-text databases** list articles and other documents and briefly summarize each item. In addition, they provide entire texts of most items indexed. Examples: *Academic Search Premier, Academic Universe, ArticleFirst, InfoTrac OneFile, Health Reference Center Academic.*

- **Databases containing abstracts** provide brief summaries of a document's content and sometimes full texts of selected items. Some provide electronic links to a library's online subscription to a journal or magazine. Examples: *PsycINFO, Sociological Abstracts, Biological Abstracts, MEDLINE, MLA Bibliography, Historical Abstracts, ERIC.*

- **Indexing or bibliographic databases** provide titles and publication (or access) information for articles and documents in a specialized field. Examples: *Art Index, GEOBASE.*

- **Resource databases** either provide access to information, images, and documents arranged in the form of an electronic reference work, or they offer tools for researchers. Examples: *WorldCat* (library and Internet resources worldwide); *Web of Science* (citation indexes identifying sources used by researchers); *RefWorks* (help with documentation styles in wide range of academic and technical fields).

10 | Finding Web and Internet Resources

Many writers conduct significant portions of their research on the Web or through Internet discussion groups. They do so because the available resources are varied, current, and easily accessible. Online texts are often shorter and less detailed than print sources, however, and many are not subjected to the same kinds of review and editorial processes as print texts. Critical evaluation, an important part of all research, is even more important when you review Web and Internet texts.

10a Developing an online search strategy

In addition to a general search strategy (8e), you should develop an online search strategy to emphasize diversity in the online sources you consult. Diversity provides contrasting perspectives and varied information.

STRATEGY **Create a planning list for electronic resources.**

Use the following list to help identify varied electronic resources.

- Web sites
- Online versions of printed texts
- Online databases (9c–d)
- Online collections of documents
- Discussion groups and newsgroups
- Visual and audio documents
- Links to Web sites

10b Finding Web and Internet resources

You can access Web documents (**pages**) or collections of pages (**sites**) using a **browser,** such as *Internet Explorer* or *Netscape Navigator.* Enter the Web page's address (a **URL** or Uniform Resource Locator), or follow links in an online text. The **Internet** links researchers through email, discussion groups, and Web sites. Materials range from well-researched reports to hasty messages. See 11d for help evaluating these sources.

Search engines. To locate sites relevant to your research, use a **search engine** that gathers data about Web sites and discussion groups. **General search engines** typically search for resources according to keywords or phrases you identify. Each search engine typically employs a different principle of selection; as a general rule, use more than one search engine to identify relevant resources.

GENERAL SEARCH ENGINES

Google	<http://www.google.com>
AltaVista	<http://altavista.com>
Yahoo!	<http://www.yahoo.com>
AllTheWeb	<http://alltheweb.com/>
Wisenut	<http://wisenut.com>
Lycos	<http://www.lycos.com>
Teoma	<http://www.teoma.com/>
HotBot	<http://hotbot.com/>

Metasearch sites enable you to conduct your search using several search engines simultaneously—and then to compare the results.

METASEARCH SITES

Dogpile	<http://dogpile.com>
Momma	<http://www.momma.com>
Metacrawler	<http://metacrawler.com>
Profusion	<http://www.profusion.com>

Electronic messages and postings. Electronic mail (**email**) allows you to contact people who can answer questions or provide information. Search engines have directory services that can locate email addresses of individuals, and many Web pages let you email the author or sponsor.

Newsgroups and **Web discussion forums** are public sites. Anyone can post messages and read other posts. In contrast, you subscribe to **electronic mailing lists** and then check your email for messages. All these sources are conversational and may or may not supply reliable information.

10c Searching efficiently

Select the terms you submit to search engines and indexes carefully. Be ready to revise them.

- Use your research questions and keywords to select search terms.
- Search engines find the exact words you specify. Type—and spell—carefully. Try various word forms and related terms.
- If a database contains items with keywords matching your search terms, the items will appear as your search results.
- Repeat a successful search, looking for other useful keywords and combinations. Use your most effective clusters to search additional databases.

A string of keywords or specific terms is called a **query.** Use your query to narrow a search by grouping terms, specifying those you want to combine, rule out, or treat as alternatives.

STRATEGY **Use advanced search strategies.**

If your search produces too many or too few items, try the advanced search strategies for the search engine or index. Many use these markers.

OR (expands): Search for either term
X OR Y → documents referring to either X or Y
AND (restricts): Search for both terms
X AND Y → documents referring to both X and Y
NOT (excludes): Search for X unless X includes Y
X NOT Y → documents referring to X unless they refer to Y

Search engines may automatically combine terms when you enter more than one word (*college drinking policy*) or ask you to use signs (*college + alcohol*) or words (*early childhood education NOT Head Start*).

10d Using Web resources

To make effective use of Web resources, you should be able to recognize some important kinds of Web sites and understand their uses.

- **Individual Web sites** are maintained by individuals but are not necessarily *about* these individuals, though they may be *home pages* created to share their lives, interests, or research. Some sites gather accounts of thoughts and actions (**blogs**) in newsworthy settings.
- **Advocacy Web sites** promote an organization's beliefs and policies. Although they favor the organization's position, many explain positions, answer critics, and provide detailed supporting evidence and documentation.
- **Informational Web sites** focus on a subject, such as sleep research, horror movies, or poetry from the 1950s Beat Generation. Their reliability varies, but the best are clearly organized, informative, and trustworthy.
- **Research-oriented Web sites,** sponsored by universities, research institutes, or professional organizations, typically contain (1) full texts of research reports, (2) summaries, (3) downloadable data in tables and graphs, (4) reviews of current research, (5) texts of unpublished papers and presentations, and (6) bibliographies of books, articles, or links.

STRATEGY **Assess your Web and Internet sources.**

The readers you address may vary in their response to your sources. Academic readers expect you to find authoritative sites produced by people aware of scholarly discussions. Public readers expect you to use sites with reliable information. Workplace readers expect you to use sites known for accuracy. Ask questions like those below to help decide how authoritative, current, or verifiable your resources are.

- How would you classify this source? Is it an individual, informational, advocacy, or research-oriented site, or something else?
- Does the site name its author or sponsor? Does the sponsor have a reputation for accuracy or expertise?
- If the item is a blog, an email message, or posting, does its author seem to have expertise? Is its argument logical and its evidence reasonable?
- Is the information credible? Does the site provide supporting evidence, alternatives, and complexities?

11 | Reading and Evaluating Sources

Research draws on reading in these ways: to gather information and ideas, to synthesize ideas and develop insights, and to evaluate sources.

11a Summarizing and paraphrasing

Summarize or paraphrase a source to put its ideas in forms useful for writing. A **summary** presents these ideas in compressed form.

STRATEGY Summarize a source.

- **Read** carefully, underlining, highlighting, or noting key ideas, supporting evidence, and other information.
- **Scan** (reread quickly) to decide which ideas and information are most important. Identify the major purpose and sections of the selection.
- **Sum up** the key ideas of *each section* in *one sentence*.
- **Capture the main point** of the *entire passage* in *one sentence*.
- **Combine** your section summaries with your overall summary .
- **Revise** for clarity. Check against the source for accuracy.
- **Document** your source using a standard style (see Part 3).

Summer Arrigo-Nelson and Jennifer Figliozzi used summary sentences to introduce a research question, noting sources in APA style (see 14a–c).

First, research has shown that adolescents who have close relationships with parents use alcohol less often than do those with conflictual relationships (Sieving, 1996). For example, a survey of students in grades 7 to 12 reported that about 35% were under parental supervision while drinking (Department of Education, 1993).

A **paraphrase** presents the content of a source in your own words with your own focus and helps you integrate the source with your ideas.

> **STRATEGY** Paraphrase a source.
>
> - **Read** carefully to understand both the wording and the content.
> - **Write** a draft using your own words in place of the original. You may retain names, proper nouns, and the like from the original.
> - **Revise** for smooth reading and clarity.
> - **Document** your source clearly using a standard style (see Part 3).

Jennifer Figliozzi read this passage in a *Chronicale of Higher Education* article on current alcohol abuse programs at various schools:

> The university also now notifies parents when their sons or daughters violate the alcohol policy, or any other aspect of the student code of conduct. "We were hoping that the support of parents would help change students' behavior, and we believe it has," says Timothy H. Brooks, an assistant vicepresident and the dean of students.

To integrate this information smoothly, Jennifer combined a paraphrase with a brief quotation and cited it using APA style (see 14a–c).

> Officials at the University of Delaware thought that letting parents know when students violate regulations on alcohol use would alter students' drinking habits, and one administrator now says, "we believe it has" (Reisberg, 1998, p. A42).

11b Synthesizing and questioning

When you synthesize several sources, you explore connections among their conclusions, evidence, and perspectives. When you question and interpret your sources, you go beyond them to develop ideas and insights of your own.

A **synthesis** can identify and relate the ideas in several sources, build links to your research question, or investigate differences among sources.

> **STRATEGY**   **Synthesize sources to highlight their relationships.**
> * **Gather and read** your sources.
> * **Focus** on the purpose and role of your synthesis, and draft a sentence summing up your conclusion about the relationship of the sources.
> * **Arrange** the order for presenting your sources in the synthesis.
> * **Write** a draft synthesis, presenting summaries of sources, offering your conclusion about the relationships, and acknowledging contradictions.
> * **Revise** for smooth reading and clear identification of sources.
> * **Document** your sources clearly using a standard style (see Part 3).

Kimlee Cunningham used this analytical synthesis to expand her paper's key ideas on the history of women's roles in Disney films. She followed MLA style, citing a one-page article and an online posting (see 13 a–c).

> It is probably an exaggeration to say that a character like Belle in <u>Beauty and the Beast</u> is a lot like a contemporary feminist, as one critic suggests (Showalter). However, we should not simply ignore an interpretation like this. Even if many people view a film like <u>Beauty and the Beast</u> (or <u>Aladdin</u>) as a simple love story (Hoffman), the films nonetheless grow out of the complicated values and roles that shape relationships today. Disney's contemporary portrayal of women characters shows a willingness to change with the times but also a reluctance to abandon traditional values and stereotypes.

As you read, you may raise questions about the ideas and information in a source—questions worth sharing with readers. Consider gathering these questions into a **problem paragraph.**

> **STRATEGY**   **Create a problem paragraph.**
> Challenge a source in a **problem paragraph** that notes problems or limitations.

Lily Germaine prepared this note card on bodybuilding.

> Tucker, pp. 389-91   Weight training & self-concept
>
> Tucker uses "although" at least four times when summarizing other studies. He's nice on the surface but sets his readers up to find fault with other studies that lack objective methodology. But he thinks he can be completely objective about such a slippery thing as "self-concept." I really question this.

Lily's problem paragraph incorporated her insights.

> Does bodybuilding affect self-concept? Before we can answer this question, we need to ask if we can accurately measure such a slippery thing as "self-concept." Some researchers, like Tucker, believe that self-concept can be accurately gauged by mathematical measurements and rigid definitions of terms. For several reasons, however, this assumption is questionable.

As you present the ideas and information in your sources, you should also interpret them and assess their value in answering a research question.

STRATEGY   Interpret and assess a source.

- State your source's conclusions accurately.
- State your own viewpoint with supporting evidence.
- Add your interpretations and conclusions.
- Assess the value and accuracy of a source. Look for reasonable judgments supported with examples and for analysis of texts or data.

11c Evaluating sources critically

Bring some healthy skepticism to *all* your print and electronic sources to be sure each is *authoritative* and to figure out any slant, or *bias*.

Evaluating sources for credibility. Printed materials can be written by uncredentialed people or can bypass certain review processes (compare the *New York Times* with, say, the *National Enquirer*), yet most published books and articles reflect the efforts of careful reviewers, editors, and publishers. In comparison, on the Internet, *anyone* can present bogus information as if it's reliable, accurate, or based on sound research.

STRATEGY   **Evaluate the credibility of your sources.**

- Who or what is the source? What can you tell about its trustworthiness and authority? Is it located at a reputable site?
- What are the author's credentials or affiliation?
- What processes has the source likely gone through to reach publication? Were there reviewers or an editorial board?
- Does the source meet the standards of your research community?
- Is the source grounded on prior research or credible authorities?
- Does the source document information, quotations, and ideas or clearly attribute them to the author?
- Does the source rely on outdated research or material?

Evaluating sources for bias. Scholarly and academic communities pride themselves on objectivity, and materials they produce are checked for balance. Still, every source has its point of view. Some sources that *appear* to be highly academic are sponsored by companies or organizations promoting a product or perspective, and they may knowingly "gear" the material in favor of that purpose.

STRATEGY   **Evaluate the bias or possible slant of your sources.**

- Does the publisher, publication, or sponsor have a reputation for balance or strong advocacy? Do other sources find the author fair?
- How accurate is the source? Does it use facts? Are its ideas generally consistent with those in other sources? Are they insightful or misleading?
- How does the writer support statements? Do claims exceed the facts?

- Does the source cite experts with political or financial interests? Does it try to hide its viewpoint?

11d Evaluating online sources critically

These Web pages show how to examine a Web site critically.

"The Good, the Bad and the Ugly: or, Why It's a Good Idea to
    Evaluate Web Sources," <http://lib.nmsu.edu/instruction/eval.html>
"Thinking Critically about World Wide Web Resources," <http://www
    .library.ucla.edu/libraries/college/help/critical/index.htm>
"Evaluating Web Resources" <http://www2.widener.edu/
    Wolfgram-Memorial-Library/webevaluation/webeval.htm>

To evaluate Web sources, ask the questions developed by Paula Mathieu and Ken McAllister for the CRITT (Critical Resources in Teaching with Technology) project at the University of Illinois at Chicago.

- **Who benefits? What difference does that make?** These questions can alert you to the perspective of the source and its effect on accuracy or trustworthiness. The Web pages at <http://www.got-milk.com/better/>, for example, seem dedicated to the reader's health (Figure 11.1). But because this site promotes drinking milk and eating milk products every day, milk processors will also benefit from sales.
- **Who's talking? What difference does that make?** These questions help you assess reliability and the likelihood of balance or bias. The "speaker" for the site's positive facts about milk is identified as "us" in the invitation to request more information. The site is linked to another page, however, that identifies the sponsor as MilkPEP (Milk Processor Education Program), sponsored by milk processors. The site is administered by the International Dairy Foods Association. What might be the point of view of these groups? Will all the "facts" appear, especially any that question milk's goodness?

In contrast, the Web page at <http://www.niddk.nih.gov/health/digest/pubs/lactose/lactose.htm> (see Figure 11.2 on p. 52) clearly and impartially answers questions about lactose intolerance, a widespread

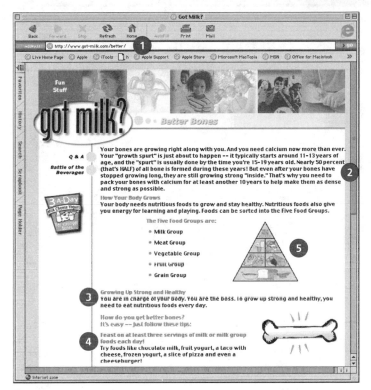

1. Commercial site
2. Links milk and milk products to healthy bones
3. Offers diet and exercise advice
4. Advocates drinking milk
5. Uses visuals to convey information

READER'S REACTION: Why are you sharing all this? How do you benefit? How do I know this is accurate, complete information?

FIGURE 11.1 "Got Milk?" Web page

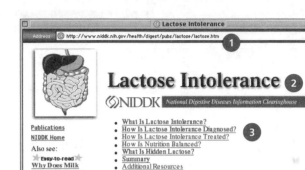

Lactose Intolerance ②

⊘NIDDK *National Digestive Diseases Information Clearinghouse*

Publications
NIDDK Home

Also see:
★ **Easy-to-read** ★
Why Does Milk Bother Me?
④

- What Is Lactose Intolerance?
- How Is Lactose Intolerance Diagnosed?
- How Is Lactose Intolerance Treated?
- How Is Nutrition Balanced?
- What Is Hidden Lactose?
- Summary
- Additional Resources
③

What Is Lactose Intolerance?

Lactose intolerance is the inability to digest significant amounts of lactose, the predominant sugar of milk. This inability results from a shortage of the enzyme lactase, which is normally produced by the cells that line the small intestine. Lactase breaks down milk sugar into simpler forms that can then be absorbed into the bloodstream. When there is not enough lactase to digest the amount of lactose consumed, the results, although not usually dangerous, may be very distressing. While not all persons deficient in lactase have symptoms, those who do are considered to be lactose intolerant.

Common symptoms include nausea, cramps, bloating, gas, and diarrhea, which begin about 30 minutes to 2 hours after eating or drinking foods containing lactose. The severity of symptoms varies depending on the amount of lactose each individual can tolerate.

Some causes of lactose intolerance are well known. For instance, certain digestive diseases and injuries to the small intestine can reduce the amount of enzymes produced. In rare

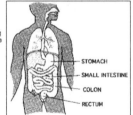

The digestive tract

cases, children are born without the ability to produce lactase. For most people, though, lactase deficiency is a condition that develops naturally over time. After about the age of 2 years, the body begins to produce less lactase. However, many people may not experience symptoms until they are much older.

---

① Government site
② Identifies topic in title
③ Uses questions and answers to explain
④ Supplies link to consumer information
⑤ Adds informative graphics

READER'S REACTION: This explanation is very clear. The sponsor is identified, too.

FIGURE 11.2 "Lactose Intolerance" Web page

inability to digest milk sugar. The "speaker" is an authoritative government agency—the National Digestive Diseases Information Clearinghouse, part of the National Institutes of Health.

- **What's missing? What difference does that make?** The *Got Milk* site is a commercial venture promoting cow's milk. Naturally it ignores soy, goat, and other milk (and nonmilk) options. On the other hand, "Lactose Intolerance" does not promote or attack dairy products; instead, its reliable advice ignores commercial and other interests. Each of these Web sites—like every other resource—has a point of view or vested interest that guides its selection and presentation of information.

11e Turning inquiry into writing

After you locate (see 9b–d) and read (see 1b and 11a–b) useful sources, you're ready to pull your research together and think strategically. Take the following steps.

- Consider what you want your readers to learn, do, or feel.
- Place your research questions in a trial sequence. Refine them.
- State, extend, and modify your rough thesis. Try breaking it into easy-to-read sentences or restating it to help readers follow your reasoning. (See 2a–b.)
- Analyze and respond to your readers' possible reactions.
- Group your materials and arrange them in sequence—beginning, middle, and end. Connect the chunks.
- Try drafting your introduction and conclusion first, focusing on your research questions. Engage readers; keep them thinking.
- Draft the middle so readers can follow your reasoning, see your evidence, and accept your conclusions. Don't just pack in details.
- Ask readers to respond to a draft. Revise, edit, proofread (1c), and design your document (see 6a–d). Quote accurately, cite page numbers and authors correctly, and check your documentation form (Part 3).

12 | Integrating and Crediting Sources

By distinguishing your contributions from those of your sources, you'll get credit for your insights and hard work. You'll also avoid inadvertently taking credit for the work of others—a form of theft called **plagiarism.** Carefully citing sources adds to your credibility, substantiates your knowledge, and allows readers to draw on your research.

12a Documenting sources for your audience

Each community of readers and writers has its own expectations about using sources.

Academic. Academic readers generally expect you to acknowledge prior work, showing how your ideas fit into a research tradition. They look for authoritative evidence and documentation appropriate to the field of research. Try to integrate sources—emphasizing quotations, findings, currency, or other matters—to meet the expectations of readers in a field.

Work. Readers at work expect brief treatment of what they know and extended treatment of what they don't (but need to). They may expect quotations, paraphrases, summaries, or visuals—all documented.

Public. Public readers may appreciate source material but be content with informal citations. But when you advocate a policy or offer controversial interpretations, readers expect fair play and accurate detail.

12b Using quotations

Select any quotation carefully, identify your source, retain its exact wording, and integrate it to support your points.

> ### POSSIBLE CONTRIBUTIONS OF QUOTATIONS
> - Bolster your conclusions with a recognized authority.
> - Convey ideas accurately, stylishly, concisely, or persuasively.
> - Provide a jumping-off point, change of pace, or vivid example.

You can quote entire sentences, with proper attribution.

> Celebrities can also play roles in our fantasy lives: "Many people admire, but do not mimic, the audacity of the rebellious rock star" (McVey 32).

Or you can embed a quotation of a few words or lines.

> Many teens were "riveted by Dylan's lyrical cynicism" (Low 124).

Guidelines for using quotations. Here are general guidelines.

- Put the exact spoken or written words of your source in quotation marks. Introduce and connect the quotation smoothly, interpreting for readers. Mention the source in your text or a citation.
- Use a colon only after an introductory line that is a complete sentence. Use commas to set off tags such as "*X* said" that introduce or interrupt a quotation. Otherwise, use the context to determine the punctuation.
- Review related conventions: combining marks (40h), capitals (35b), and brackets and ellipses (40c–d).
- If you use a specific documentation style (see Part 3), check its advice on quotations and in-text citations

Block quotations for prose. When you quote a passage longer than four lines typed (MLA style) or forty words or more (APA style), begin on the line after your introduction. Indent 1" or ten spaces (MLA style, see 13c) or 1/2" or five spaces (APA style, shown below, and see 14c). Double-space but omit quotation marks (unless they appear in the source).

Perez (1998) anticipates shifts in staff training:

> The great challenge for most school districts is to earmark
> sufficient funds for training personnel, not for purchasing or
> upgrading hardware and software. The technological revolution
> in the average classroom will depend to a large degree on
> innovation in professional development. (p. 64)

Begin the first line without further indentation if you quote from one paragraph. Otherwise, indent all paragraphs 1/4" or three spaces (MLA) or any additional paragraph 1/2" or five spaces (APA).

Block quotations for poetry. When you quote four or more lines of poetry, begin on the line after your introduction. Indent 1" or ten spaces from the left (MLA style, shown below). Double-space, and don't use quotation marks unless the verse contains them.

Donald Hall also varies line length and rhythm, as "The Black-Faced Sheep" illustrates.

> My grandfather spent all day searching the valley
> and edges of Ragged Mountain,
> calling "Ke-<u>day</u>!" as if he brought you salt,
> "Ke-<u>day</u>! Ke-<u>day</u>!" (lines 9–12)

12c Integrating sources into your text

Credit your sources, and weave their points or details into your own line of reasoning. To make your writing more sophisticated, quote selectively. Paraphrase, summarize, or synthesize instead (see 11a–b).

EMBEDDING SOURCE MATERIAL

- Select sound evidence that supports your purpose and thesis.
- Alternate striking short quotations with paraphrase and summary to avoid long, tedious quotations.

- Draw facts, details, and statistics from your sources as well as ideas and expressions. Credit these, too.
- Don't just tack sources together assuming readers will figure out how to interpret or connect them. Integrate sources so your interpretation and reasoning shape the discussion.

Drawings, photos, tables, graphs, and charts can consolidate or explore data (see 6d). If you copy or download a visual, you'll need to cite its source and may need permission to use it.

STRATEGY **Integrate visuals for readers.**

- Put the visual close to the relevant text without disrupting the discussion. Make sure that it explains or extends your point.
- Use clear, readable visuals in an appropriate size.
- Add labels (MLA: Table 1, Fig. 1; APA: *Figure 1*).

12d Avoiding plagiarism

As you quote, paraphrase, or summarize, you *must* cite sources.

- Enclose someone's exact words in quotation marks.
- Paraphrase and summarize in your own words.
- Cite the source of whatever you integrate.

Without quotation marks, the following paraphrase is too close to the original and would be seen as plagiarized

ORIGINAL PASSAGE

Malnutrition was a widespread and increasingly severe problem throughout the least developed parts of the world in the 1970s, and would continue to be serious, occasionally reaching famine conditions, as the millennium approached. Among the cells of the human body most dependent upon a steady source of nutrients are those of the immune system, most of which live, even under ideal conditions, for only days at a time. (From Laurie Garrett, *The Coming Plague*, New York: Penguin, 1994, p. 199.)

PLAGIARIZED VERSION

In her book about emerging global diseases, Garrett points out that malnutrition can give microbes an advantage as they spread through the population. Malnutrition continues to be a **severe problem throughout the least developed parts of the world.** The human immune system contains cells that are **dependent upon a steady source of nutrients.** These cells may **live, even under ideal conditions, for only days at a time.**

The writer of the plagiarized version made only minor changes in some phrases and "lifted" others verbatim.

APPROPRIATE PARAPHRASE

In her book about emerging global diseases, Garrett points out that malnutrition can give microbes an advantage as they spread through the population. The human body contains immune cells that help to fight off various diseases. When the body is deprived of nutrients, these immune cells will weaken (Garrett 199).

For a paper on the general threat of global disease, the passage could simply be summarized.

APPROPRIATE SUMMARY

Malnutrition can so weaken people's immune systems that diseases they would otherwise fight off can gain an advantage (Garrett 199).

12e Deciding what to document

In general, document words, ideas, and information drawn from another person's work. Add credibility by showing your careful research, acknowledging someone's hard work, and giving others access to your sources. What needs documenting may vary with your readers. General readers may expect sources when you identify subatomic particles; physicists probably would assume this is common knowledge.

You *Must* Document
- Word-for-word (direct) quotations from a source

- Paraphrases or summaries of someone else's work, whether published or presented orally or electronically
- Ideas, opinions, and interpretations that others have developed, even those based on common knowledge
- Facts or data someone has gathered or identified, unless the information is considered common knowledge
- Information that is disputed or not widely accepted
- Visuals, recordings, performances, interviews, and the like

But *Do Not* Document
- Ideas, opinions, and interpretations that are your own
- Widely known information available in common reference works or generally seen as common knowledge
- Commonly used quotations ("To be, or not to be")

12f Presenting sources

In a traditional research paper or report you present information and ideas from your sources as part of your written text: as quotations, summaries, or paraphrases. Writers today have many more choices, however. You may begin by envisioning your paper as a stack of neatly laid out pages emerging from your computer's printer. But this is not your *only* option, nor is it necessarily your best option.

Printed document with visuals. A printed document does not have to rely on words alone, and it does not have to be regular (and perhaps unexciting) in appearance. Your word-processing program will enable you to integrate information in the form of charts, graphs, pictures, and clip art. When you incorporate visual material, make sure it adds substantial ideas and information to your work. If you can, place the visual near the relevant part of the written discussion so readers can see the relationship between them.

Presentation programs like *PowerPoint* enable you to arrange information in graphic ways that emphasize relationships and highlight key ideas. They can also incorporate action sequences like arrows linking statements

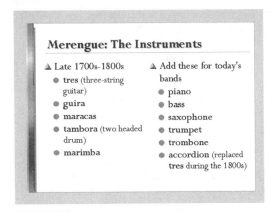

FIGURE 12.1 *PowerPoint* presentation within a document

or fades from one piece of text (or a visual) to another. Because *PowerPoint* and similar programs do not allow for the extensive presentation of text, they work best when incorporated within word-processed documents (see Figure 12.1).

Webbed document. A webbed document, a Web page or a file written in HTML, allows readers to move around at will within a document. You can include electronic links to online texts of research articles you have summarized or paraphrased, giving readers a chance to test the accuracy of your work. Or you can include links to Web sites that provide additional supporting evidence or arguments. If you plan to create such a document, write each section so that it can be understood more or less on its own because Web documents are rarely read in a conventionally linear way.

Voices
from the Community

"The MLA Handbook for Writers of Research Papers is designed to introduce you to the customs of a community of writers who greatly value scrupulous scholarship and the careful documentation, or recording, of research."

—Joseph Gibaldi, *MLA Handbook for Writers of Research Papers,* 6th ed.

"Rules for the preparation of manuscripts should contribute to clear communication. . . . They spare readers a distracting variety of forms throughout a work and permit readers to give full attention to content."

—*Publication Manual of the American Psychological Association,* 5th ed., p. xxiii

GUIDE TO MLA FORMATS

MLA Formats for In-Text (Parenthetical) Citations

MLA Formats for List of Works Cited

13 | MLA Style

The MLA (Modern Language Association) documentation style is a clear system for acknowledging your sources and directing readers to them. It has two elements: a citation in the text (usually in parentheses) and a list of works cited (at the end of the text).

These elements are simple and direct in MLA style, which emphasizes scrupulous respect for ideas, information, and quotations from sources. Use it in academic settings when you write in a humanities field or your instructor asks for simple, parenthetical documentation. Consider it in public and work settings when your audience would appreciate a clear, direct style that seldom uses footnotes or endnotes.

For more detailed discussion, see the *MLA Handbook for Writers of Research Papers* (6th ed., New York: MLA, 2003), the *MLA Style Manual and Guide to Scholarly Publishing* (2nd ed., New York: MLA, 1998), or updates posted on the MLA Web site <http://www.mla.org/style/style_faq>.

13a MLA in-text (parenthetical) citations

In MLA style, you include in the text information that helps readers identify and locate your source, described in full in the list of works cited at the end of the paper. Generally, an author's name is enough to identify the source. Provide this basic information in one of two places: in parentheses or in your discussion.

1. Author's Name in Parentheses

IN PARENTHESES When people marry now, "there is an important sense in which

they don't know what they are doing" (Giddens 46).

2. Author's Name in Discussion

IN DISCUSSION   Giddens claims that when people marry now "there is an

important sense in which they don't know what they are

doing" (46).

3. General Reference

A **general reference** refers to ideas or information throughout the source as a whole; it needs no page number.

IN PARENTHESES   Many species of animals have complex systems of

communication (Bright).

IN DISCUSSION   As Michael Bright observes, many species of animals have

complex systems of communication.

4. Specific Reference

A **specific reference** documents words, ideas, or facts from a particular place in a source, such as the page from which you draw a quotation or paraphrase.

QUOTATION   Dolphins perceive clicking sounds "made up of 700 units of

sound per second" (Bright 52).

PARAPHRASE   Bright reports that dolphins recognize patterns consisting of

seven hundred clicks each second (52).

5. One Author

According to Maureen Honey, government posters during World War II often

portrayed homemakers "as vital defenders of the nation's homes" (135).

6. Two or Three Authors

The item is noted in a partial list of Francis Bacon's debts from 1603 on

(Jardine and Stewart 275).

Follow the same pattern for three authors: (Norman, Fraser, and Jenko 209).

7. More Than Three Authors

Within parentheses, use *et al.* ("and others") after the name of the first author. Within your discussion, use phrases like "Chen and his colleagues observe." If you give all the names in the works cited list rather than using *et al.*, do the same in the text (see Entry 3, p. 71).

> More funding would encourage creative research on complementary
>
> medicine (Chen et al. 1982).

8. Corporate or Group Author

If an organization is named as the author, use its name in the text or the citation; shorten cumbersome names such as Committee of Concerned Journalists.

> The consortium gathers American journalists at "a critical moment"
>
> (Committee 187).

9. No Author Given

> In 1993, Czechoslovakia split into the Czech Republic and the Slovak
>
> Republic (<u>Baedeker's</u> 67).

The full title is *Baedeker's Czech/Slovak Republics.*

10. More Than One Work by the Same Author

When the list of works cited contains more than one entry by an author, add a shortened title to your citation.

> One writer claims that "quaintness glorifies the unassuming
>
> industriousness" in these social classes (Harris, <u>Cute</u> 46).

11. Authors with the Same Name

Add the first initial or name to distinguish the author.

> Despite improved health information systems (J. Adams 308), medical
>
> errors continue to increase (D. Adams 1).

12. Indirect Source

Use *qtd. in* ("quoted in") for a quotation or paraphrase taken from yet another source. Here, Feuch is the source of the quotation from Vitz.

> For Vitz, "art, especially great art, must engage all or almost all of the
>
> major capacities of the nervous system" (qtd. in Feuch 65).

13. Multivolume Work

To cite a whole volume, add a comma after the author's name and *vol.* before the number (Cao, vol. 4). To specify one of several volumes that you cite, add the volume number to the text citation (Cao 4: 177).

> In 1888, Lewis Carroll gave two students permission to call their school
>
> paper <u>Jabberwock</u>, a made-up word from <u>Alice's Adventures in</u>
>
> <u>Wonderland</u> (Cohen 2: 695).

14. Literary Work

After the page number in your edition, add the chapter (*ch.*), part (*pt.*), or section (*sec.*) number to help readers find the passage in other editions.

> In <u>Huckleberry Finn</u>, Mark Twain ridicules an actor who "would squeeze
>
> his hand on his forehead and stagger back and kind of moan" (178; ch. 21).

For poems, give line numbers (lines 55–57) or both part and line numbers (4.220–23). For plays, give act, scene, and line numbers: (<u>Ham.</u> 1.2.76).

15. Bible

Place a period between the chapter and verse (Mark 2.3–4). In parenthetical citations, abbreviate names with five or more letters, such as Deuteronomy: (Deut. 16.21–22).

16. Selection in Anthology

For an essay, story, poem, or other selection in an anthology, cite the work's author (not the anthology's editor), but give page numbers in the anthology.

> According to Corry, the battle for Internet censorship has crossed party
>
> lines (112).

17. Two or More Sources in a Citation

Separate sources within a citation with a semicolon.

> The different ways men and women use language can often be traced to
>
> who has power (Tanner 83-86; Tavris 297-301).

18. Electronic or Other Nonprint Source

Identify the author or title needed to find the entry in your list of works cited. Add numbers for the page, paragraph (*par., pars.*), section (*sec.*), or screen (*screen*) if given. Otherwise, no number is needed.

> Offspringmag.com summarizes current research on adolescent behavior
>
> (Boynton screen 2).

> The heroine's mother in the film Clueless died as the result of an
>
> accident during liposuction.

19. Informative Footnote or Endnote

When you wish to comment on a source or supply lengthy information useful to only a few readers, use a footnote or endnote. Place a superscript

---

PLACEMENT AND PUNCTUATION OF PARENTHETICAL CITATIONS

Put parenthetical citations close to the quotation, information, para-phrase, or summary you are documenting.

- At the end of a sentence before the final punctuation

  Wayland Hand reports on a folk belief that going to sleep on a rug

  made of bearskin can relieve backache (183).

- After the part of the sentence to which the citation applies, at a nat-ural pause in the sentence so that you do not disrupt it, or after the last of several quotations in a paragraph, all from one page of the same source

  The folk belief that "sleeping on a bear rug will cure backache" (Hand

  183) illustrates the magic of external objects producing results inside

  the body.

- At the end of a long quotation set off as a block (see 12b), after the end punctuation with a space before the parentheses

  Many baseball players are superstitious, especially pitchers.

  > Some pitchers refuse to walk anywhere on the day of the
  >
  > game in the belief that every little exertion subtracts from
  >
  > their playing strength. One pitcher would never put on his
  >
  > cap until the game started and would not wear it at all on
  >
  > the days he did not pitch. (Gmelch 280)

---

number (raised slightly above the line of text) at a suitable point in your paper. Then provide the note itself, with a corresponding number, as a footnote at the end of the page or as an endnote at the paper's end, before the list of works cited, on a page titled "Notes," as in the following example.

[1] Before changing your eating habits or beginning an exercise program, check with your doctor.

13b MLA list of works cited

Provide readers with detailed publication information about the sources you cite in your text.

- Begin a list titled "Works Cited" on a new page right after your paper ends. If you include all the works you consulted, not just those you cited, call it "Works Consulted." (See p. 90 for a sample list.)
- Alphabetize by authors' last names; then alphabetize multiple works by the same author by title. For sources without authors, use the first main word in the title.
- Do not indent the first line of each entry; indent additional lines one-half inch or five spaces.
- Double-space the entire list. Consistently leave a single space (as in print) or two spaces (if used in your text) after a period within an entry.

Books and Works Treated as Books

Provide the author's name (last name first); underlined title; city of publication, publisher in short form (*U of Chicago P* for University of Chicago Press or *McGraw* for *McGraw-Hill, Inc.*), and year of publication.

1. One Author

Hockney, David. <u>Secret Knowledge: Recovering the Lost Techniques of the Old Masters.</u> New York: Viking Studio, 2001.

2. Two or Three Authors

Kress, Gunther, and Theo van Leeuwen. <u>Reading Images: The Grammar of Graphic Design.</u> London: Routledge, 1996.

3. Four or More Authors

After the first name, add *et al.* (meaning "and others").

> Bellah, Robert N., et al. <u>Habits of the Heart: Individualism and</u>
>
>   <u>Commitment in American Life</u>. Berkeley: U of California P, 1985.

You also may give all the names; if so, list them in any parenthetical citations (see Entry 7, p. 66).

4. Corporate or Group Author

If the organization is also the publisher, repeat its name, abbreviated if appropriate.

> Nemours Children's Clinic. <u>Diabetes and Me</u>. Wilmington, DE: Nemours,
>
>   2001.

5. No Author Given

> <u>Guide for Authors</u>. Oxford: Blackwell, 1985.

6. More Than One Work by the Same Author

> Tannen, Deborah. <u>The Argument Culture: Moving from Debate to Dialogue</u>.
>
>   New York: Random, 1998.
>
>   . <u>You Just Don't Understand: Women and Men in Conversation</u>.
>
>   New York: Ballantine, 1991.

7. One or More Editors

> Achebe, Chinua, and C. L. Innes, eds. <u>African Short Stories</u>. London:
>
>   Heinemann, 1985.

8. Author and Editor

Wardlow, Gayle Dean. Chasin' That Devil Music: Searching for the Blues. Ed.

Edward Komara. San Francisco: Miller, 1998.

9. Translator

Baudrillard, Jean. Cool Memories II: 1978-1990. Trans. Chris Turner.

Durham: Duke UP, 1996.

10. Edition Following the First

Coe, Michael D. The Maya. 6th ed. New York: Thames, 1999.

11. Reprint

Ishiguro, Kazuo. A Pale View of Hills. 1982. New York: Vintage Intl.,

1990.

12. Multivolume Work

You may cite the whole work or a specific volume, ending with the total volumes or the full range of dates, if you wish.

Tsao, Hsueh-chin. The Story of the Stone. Trans. David Hawkes.

5 vols. Harmondsworth, Eng.: Penguin, 1983-86.

Tsao, Hsueh-chin. The Story of the Stone. Trans. David Hawkes. Vol. 1.

Harmondsworth, Eng.: Penguin, 1983. 5 vols.

13. Work in a Series

Hess, Gary R. Vietnam and the United States: Origins and Legacy of War.

Intl. Hist. Ser. 7. Boston: Twayne, 1990.

14. Book Pre-1900

Darwin, Charles. <u>Descent of Man and Selection in Relation to Sex</u>.

     New York, 1896.

15. Book with Publisher's Imprint

Sikes, Gini. <u>8 Ball Chicks: A Year in the Violent World of Girl Gangs</u>.

     New York: Anchor-Doubleday, 1997.

Anchor is the imprint.

16. Anthology or Collection of Articles

Wu, Duncan, ed. <u>Romantic Women Poets: An Anthology</u>. Oxford: Blackwell,

     1997.

To cite a specific selection, see Entry 34, page 76.

17. Conference Proceedings

<u>Childhood Obesity: Causes and Prevention</u>. Symposium Proc.,

     27 Oct. 1998. Washington: Center for Nutrition Policy and Promotion,

     1999.

18. Title Within a Title

Weick, Carl F. <u>Refiguring</u> Huckleberry Finn. Athens: U of Georgia P,

     2000.

Golden, Catherine, ed. <u>The Captive Imagination: A Casebook on "The</u>

     <u>Yellow Wall-paper."</u> New York: Feminist, 1992.

19. Pamphlet

Vareika, William. John La Farge: An American Master (1835-1910).

> Newport: Gallery of American Art, 1989.

20. Dissertation (Published)

Said, Edward W. Joseph Conrad and the Fiction of Autobiography. Diss.

> Harvard U, 1964. Cambridge: Harvard UP, 1966.

21. Dissertation (Unpublished)

Swope, Catherine Theodora. "Redesigning Downtown: The Fabrication of

> German-Themed Villages in Small-Town America." Diss. U of

> Washington, 2003.

22. Government Document

Sheppard, David I., and Shay Bilchick, comps. Promising Strategies to

> Reduce Gun Violence Report. US Dept. of Justice. Office of Juvenile

> Justice and Delinquency Prevention. Washington: GPO, 1999.

United States. Cong. House. Anti-Spamming Act of 2001. 107th Cong., 1st

> sess. Washington: GPO, 2001.

Articles from Periodicals and Selections from Books

Provide the author's name (last name first), article title (in quotation marks), book or periodical title (underlined), and publication information (volume number for a periodical, date, page numbers). When the pages are not consecutive, give the first one with a + (48+).

23. Article in Journal Paginated by Volume

When each volume consists of several issues with continuous pagination through them all, supply the volume number.

Rockwood, Bruce L. "Law, Literature, and Science Fiction: New

Possibilities." <u>Legal Studies Forum</u> 23 (1999): 267-80.

24. Article in Journal Paginated by Issue

When each issue begins with page 1, add the issue number after the volume number.

Adams, Jessica. "Local Color: The Southern Plantation in Popular Culture."

<u>Cultural Critique</u> 42.1 (1999): 171-87.

25. Article in Weekly Magazine

Conlin, Michelle. "Unmarried America." <u>Business Week</u> 20 Oct. 2003:

106+.

26. Article in Monthly Magazine

Jacobson, Doranne. "Doing Lunch." <u>Natural History</u> Mar. 2000: 66-69.

27. Article with No Author Given

"The Obesity Industry." <u>Economist</u> 27 Sept. 2003: 64+.

28. Article in Newspaper

For a local newspaper, add the city's name in brackets after the title unless the city is named in the title.

Willis, Ellen. "Steal This Myth: Why We Still Try to Re-create the Rush of

the 60's." <u>New York Times</u> 20 Aug. 2000: AR1+.

29. Editorial

"A False Choice." Editorial. <u>Charlotte Observer</u> 16 Aug. 1998: 2C.

30. Letter to the Editor

Larson, Dea. Letter. <u>Wall Street Journal</u> 28 Oct. 2003: A17.

31. Interview (Published)

Stewart, Martha. "'I Do Have a Brain.'" Interview with Kevin Kelly. <u>Wired</u>
Aug. 1998: 114.

32. Review

Include the reviewer and the review's title, if available.

Muñoz, José Esteban. "Citizens and Superheroes." Rev. of <u>The Queen of</u>
<u>America Goes to Washington City</u>, by Lauren Berlant. <u>American</u>
<u>Quarterly</u> 52 (2000): 397-404.

Hadjor, Kofi Buenor. Rev. of <u>The Silent War: Imperialism and the</u>
<u>Changing Perception of Race</u>, by Frank Furendi. <u>Journal of Black</u>
<u>Studies</u> 30 (1999): 133-35.

33. Article in Encyclopedia or Reference Work

Oliver, Paul, and Barry Kernfeld. "Blues." <u>The New Grove Dictionary of</u>
<u>Jazz</u>. Ed. Barry Kernfeld. New York: St. Martin's, 1994.

"The History of Western Theatre." <u>The New Encyclopaedia Britannica:</u>
<u>Macropedia</u>. 15th ed. 1987. Vol. 28.

34. Chapter in Edited Book or Selection in Anthology

Atwood, Margaret. "Bluebeard's Egg." <u>"Bluebeard's Egg" and Other Stories</u>.
New York: Fawcett-Random, 1987. 131-64.

For a reprinted selection, you may add the original source.

Atwood, Margaret. "Bluebeard's Egg." Bluebeard's Egg" and Other Stories.

New York: Fawcett-Random, 1987. 131–64. Rpt. in Don't Bet on the

Prince: Contemporary Feminist Fairy Tales in North America and

England. Ed. Jack Zipes. New York: Methuen, 1986. 160-82.

35. More Than One Selection from Anthology or Collection

Include an entry for the collection and the author's name as a basis for cross-references.

Goldberg, Jonathan. "Speculation: Macbeth and Source." Howard and

O'Connor 242-64.

Howard, Jean E., and Marion F. O'Connor, eds. Shakespeare Reproduced:

The Text in History and Ideology. New York: Methuen, 1987.

36. Preface, Foreword, Introduction, or Afterword

Tomlin, Janice. Foreword. The Complete Guide to Foreign Adoption. By

Barbara Brooke Bascom and Carole A. McKelvey. New York: Pocket,

1997.

37. Letter (Published)

Garland, Hamlin. "To Fred Lewis Pattee." 30 Dec. 1914. Letter 206 of

Selected Letters of Hamlin Garland. Ed. Keith Newlin and Joseph B.

McCullough. Lincoln: U of Nebraska P, 1998.

38. Dissertation Abstract

Hawkins, Joanne Berning. "Horror Cinema and the Avante-Garde." Diss. U.

of California, Berkeley, 1993. DAI 55 (1995): 1712A.

Field and Media Resources

39. Interview (Unpublished)

Identify the person interviewed and the type of interview: *Personal interview* (you conducted it in person), *Telephone interview* (you talked to the person over the telephone), or *Interview* (someone else conducted the interview, perhaps on radio or television).

Schutt, Robin. E-mail interview. 7 Oct. 2001.

Coppola, Francis Ford. Interview with James Lipton. Inside the Actors

Studio. Bravo, New York. 10 July 2001.

40. Survey or Questionnaire

MLA does not specify a form for these field resources. When citing your own field research, you may wish to use this format.

Figliozzi, Jennifer Emily, and Summer J. Arrigo-Nelson. Questionnaire on

Student Alcohol Use and Parental Values. U of Rhode Island,

Kingston. 15-20 Apr. 2004.

41. Observation

Because MLA does not specify a form, you may wish to cite your field notes in this way.

Ba, Ed. Ski Run Observation. Vail, CO. 26 Jan. 2004.

42. Letter or Memo (Unpublished)

Hall, Donald. Letter to the author. 24 Jan. 1990.

43. Oral Presentation

Johnson, Sylvia. "Test Fairness: An Oxymoron? The Challenge of Measuring

Well in a High Stakes Climate." Amer. Educ. Research Assn. Sheraton

Hotel, New Orleans. 27 Apr. 2000.

44. Performance

Cabaret. By Joe Masteroff. Dir. Sam Mendes. Studio 54, New York. 2 July
2001.

45. Videotape or Film

Rosencrantz and Guildenstern Are Dead. Dir. Tom Stoppard. Perf. Gary
Oldman, Tim Roth, and Richard Dreyfuss. Videocassette. Buena Vista
Home Video, 1990.

Rosencrantz and Guildenstern Are Dead. Dir. Tom Stoppard. Perf. Gary
Oldman, Tim Roth, and Richard Dreyfuss. Cinecom Entertainment,
1990.

46. Television or Radio Program

"The Tour." I Love Lucy. Dir. William Asher. Nickelodeon. 2 July
2001.

47. Recording

Identify the recording's form unless it's a compact disc.

The Goo-Goo Dolls. Dizzy Up the Girl. Warner, 1998.

Mozart, Wolfgang Amadeus. Symphony no. 40 in G minor. Vienna
Philharmonic. Cond. Leonard Bernstein. Audiocassette. Deutsche
Grammophon, 1984.

48. Artwork or Photograph

Leonardo da Vinci. Mona Lisa. Louvre, Paris.

Larimer Street, Denver. Personal photograph by author. 5 May 2004.

49. Map or Chart

<u>Arkansas</u>. Map. Comfort, TX: Gousha, 1996.

50. Comic Strip or Cartoon

Cochran, Tony. "Agnes." Comic Strip. <u>Denver Post</u> 9 May 2004: 4.

51. Advertisement

Toyota. Advertisement. <u>GQ</u> July 2001: 8.

Online and Electronic Resources

For each entry supply both the date when the material was posted (or last revised or updated) and then the date you accessed it. Note the address or URL (beginning with *http, gopher, telnet, ftp*) in angle brackets. Include the search page, links, path, or file name needed for a reader to reach the page or frame you used. Break the line only after a slash (without adding a hyphen).

52. Professional Web Site

<u>History of the American West, 1860-1920</u>. 25 July 2000. Denver Public

Lib. 16 Oct. 2001 <http://memory.loc.gov/ammem/award97/

codhtml>.

53. Academic Home Page

Baron, Dennis. Home page. 16 Aug. 2000. Dept. of English, U of Illinois,

Urbana-Champaign. 10 Oct. 2003 <http://www2.english.uiuc.edu/

baron/Default.htm>.

54. Online Book

London, Jack. The Iron Heel. New York: Macmillan, 1908. The Jack London

Collection. 10 Dec. 1999. Berkeley Digital Library SunSITE. 15 July

2001 <http://sunsite.berkeley.edu/London/Writing/IronHeel/>.

55. Selection from Online Book

Muir, John. "The City of the Saints." Steep Trails. 1918. 17 July 2001

<http://encyclopediaindex.com/b/sttrl10.htm>.

56. Online Journal Article

Dugdale, Timothy. "The Fan and (Auto)Biography: Writing the Self in the

Stars." Journal of Mundane Behavior 1.2 (2000). 19 Sept. 2000

<http://www.mundanebehavior.org/issues/v1n2/dugdale.htm>.

57. Online Magazine Article

Wright, Laura. "My, What Big Eyes . . ." Discover 27 Oct. 2003. 4 Apr. 2004

<http://www.discover.com/web-exclusives-archive/

big-eyed-trilobite1027/>.

58. Online Newspaper Article

Mulvihill, Kim. "Childhood Obesity." San Francisco Chronicle 12 July 2001.

15 July 2001 <http://www.sfgate.com/search>.

59. Online Government Document

United States. Dept. of Commerce. Bureau of the Census. Census Brief:

Disabilities Affect One-Fifth of All Americans. Dec. 1997. 18 July 2001

<http://www.census.gov/prod/3/97pubs/cenbr975.pdf>.

60. Online Editorial

"Mall Mania/A Measure of India's Success." Editorial. <u>startribune.com</u>

<u>Minneapolis-St. Paul</u> 31 Oct. 2003. 14 Nov. 2003 <http://

www.startribune.com/stories/1519/4185511.html>.

61. Online Letter to the Editor

Hadjiargyrou, Michael. "Stem Cells and Delicate Questions." Letter.

<u>New York Times on the Web</u> 17 July 2001. 18 July 2001 <http://

www.nytimes.com/2001/07/18/opinion/ L18STEM.html>.

62. Online Interview

Rikker, David. Interview with Victor Payan. <u>San Diego Latino Film Festival</u>.

May 1999. 20 Jan. 2002 <http://www.sdlatinofilm.com/

video.html#Anchor-David-64709>.

63. Online Review

Chaudhury, Parama. Rev. of <u>Kandahar</u>, dir. Mohsen Makhmalbaf. <u>Film</u>

<u>Monthly</u> 3.4 (2002). 19 Jan. 2002. <http://www.filmmonthly.com/

Playing/Articles/Kandahar/Kandahar.html>.

64. Online Abstract

Prelow, Hazel, and Charles A. Guarnaccia. "Ethnic and Racial Differences in

Life Stress among High School Adolescents." <u>Journal of Counseling &</u>

<u>Development</u> 75.6 (1997). Abstract. 6 Apr. 1998 <http://

www.counseling.org/journals/jcdjul197.htm#Prelow>.

65. Online Database: General Entry

For entries from online library databases, begin with the details of print publication, if any. Name the database, subscription service, library, and your date of access. Then give the URL for the site or, if it's long, for the site's search page. Should the service give only the first page number of the printed text, follow it with a hyphen, space, and period, as in 223-.

Kallis, Giorgos, and Henri L. F. De Groot. "Shifting Perspectives on Urban

     Water Policy in Europe." European Planning Studies 11 (2003):

     223-28. Academic Search Premier. EBSCO. Auraria Lib., Denver, CO.

     19 Dec. 2003 <http://0-web12.epnet.com.skyline.cudenver.edu>.

66. Online Database: Journal Article

Stillman, Todd. "McDonald's in Question: The Limits of the Mass Market."

     American Behavioral Scientist 47 (2003): 107-18. Academic Search

     Premier. EBSCO. U of Rhode Island Lib. 15 Nov. 2003 <http://

     0-ejournals.ebsco.com>.

67. Online Database: Article Abstract

Lewis, David A., and Roger P. Rose. "The President, the Press, and the

     War-Making Power: An Analysis of Media Coverage Prior to the

     Persian Gulf War." Presidential Studies Quarterly 32 (2002): 559-71.

     Abstract. America: History and Life. ABC/CLIO. U of Rhode Island Lib.

     1 Nov. 2003 <http://0-serials.abc-clio.com>.

68. Online Database: Magazine Article

Barrett, Jennifer. "Fast Food Need Not Be Fat Food." <u>Newsweek</u> 13 Oct.

2003: 73-74. <u>Academic Search Premier</u>. EBSCO. U of Rhode Island Lib.

31 Oct. 2003 <http://0-ejournals.ebsco.com>.

69. Online Database: Newspaper Article

Lee, R. "Class with the 'Ph.D. Diva.'" <u>New York Times</u> 18 Oct. 2003: B7.

<u>InfoTrac OneFile</u>. InfoTrac. Providence Public Lib., RI. 31 Oct. 2003

<http://infotrac.galegroup.com/menu>.

70. Online Database: Summary of Research

Holub, Tamara. "Early-Decision Programs." <u>ERIC Digests</u>. ERIC Clearinghouse

on Higher Education. ERIC, the Educational Resources Information

Center. ED470540. 2002. U of Rhode Island Lib. 7 Nov. 2003

<http://www.ericfacility.net/ericdigests/ed470540.html>.

71. Online Database: Collection of Documents

"Combating Plagiarism." <u>CQ Researcher</u> 9 Sept. 2003. CQ P. U of Rhode Island

Lib. 12 Nov. 2003 <http://0-library.cqpress.com.helin.uri.edu:80/

cqresearcher/>.

72. Online Database: Personal Subscription Service

Introduce your access route by *Keyword* or *Path*.

"Native American Food Guide." <u>Health Finder</u>. 16 July 2001. America

Online. 16 July 2001. Keyword: Health.

73. Online Videotape or Film

Coppola, Francis Ford, dir. Apocalypse Now. 1979. Film.com. 17 July 2001
   <http://ramhurl.film.com/smildemohurl.ram?file=screen/2001/clips/
   apoca.smi>.

74. Online Television or Radio Program

Edwards, Bob. "Adoption: Redefining Family." Morning Edition.
   Natl. Public Radio. 28-29 June 2001. 17 July 2001 <http://
   www.npr.org/ programs/morning/features/2001/jun/
   010628.cfoa.html>.

75. Online Recording

Malcolm X. "The Definition of Black Power." 8 Mar. 1964. Great Speeches.
   2000. 18 July 2001 <http://www.chicago-law.net/speeches/
   speech.html#1m>.

76. Online Artwork

Elamite Goddess. 2100 BC (?). Louvre, Paris. 16 July 2001 <http://
   www.louvre.fr/louvrea.htm/searchs>

77. Online Map or Chart

"Beirut [Beyrout] 1912." Map. Perry-Castañeda Library Map Collection.
   16 July 2000 <http://www.lib.utexas.edu/maps/historical/
   beirut2_1912.jpg>.

78. Online Comic Strip or Cartoon

Auth, Tony. "Spending Goals." Cartoon. <u>Slate</u> 7 Sept. 2001. 16 Oct. 2001

<http://cagle.slate.msn.com/politicalcartoons/pccartoons/archives/

auth.asp>.

79. Online Advertisement

Mazda Miata. Advertisement. 16 July 2001 <http://www.mazdausa.com/

miata/>.

80. Other Online Sources

When citing an electronic source not explained here, adapt the appropriate nonelectronic MLA model.

NASA/JPL. "Martian Meteorite." <u>Views of the Solar System: Meteoroids and

Meteorites</u>. Ed. Calvin J. Hamilton. 1999. 13 June 1999 <http://

spaceart.com/solar/eng/meteor.htm#views>.

81. FTP, Telnet, or Gopher Site

Treat a source obtained through FTP (file transfer protocol), telnet, or gopher as you would a similar Web source.

Clinton, William Jefferson. "Radio Address of the President to the Nation."

10 May 1997. 29 June 1999 <ftp://OMA.EOP.GOV.US/1997/5/10/

1.TEXT.1>.

82. Email

Give the writer's name, the title (or type) of communication, and the date.

Trimbur, John. E-mail to the author. 17 Sept. 2000.

83. Online Posting

Aid readers (if you can) by citing an archived version.

> Brock, Stephen E. "School Crisis." Online posting. 27 Apr. 2001. Special
>
> Events Chat Transcripts. Lycos Communities. 18 July 2001 <http://
>
> clubs.lycos.com/live/Events/transcripts/school_crisis_tscript.asp>.

84. Synchronous Communication

When citing material from a MUD, MOO, or other form of synchronous communication, identify the speaker, the event, its date, its forum (such as CollegeTownMOO), and your access date. End with *telnet* and the address. Cite an archived version if possible.

> Finch, Jeremy. Online debate "Can Proust Save Your Life?" 3 Apr. 1998.
>
> CollegeTownMOO. 3 Apr. 1998 <telnet://next.cs.bvc.edu.7777>.

85. CD-ROM, Diskette, or Magnetic Tape

> Shakespeare, William. All's Well That Ends Well. William Shakespeare: The
>
> Complete Works on CD-ROM. CD-ROM. Abingdon, Eng.: Andromeda
>
> Interactive, 1994.

86. CD-ROM Abstract

> Straus, Stephen. Interview with Claudia Dreifus. "Separating Remedies
>
> from Snake Oil." New York Times 3 Apr. 2001: D5+. Abstract.
>
> CD-ROM. InfoTrac. 19 July 2001.

13c MLA sample pages

The *MLA Handbook* recommends beginning a research paper with the first page of the text, using the format shown on Jenny Latimer's first page.

↑ **1/2" from top**
Latimer 1

↑ **1" from top**

Jenny Latimer   **Heading format without title page**   **1" margin on each side**

Professor Schwegler

Writing 101   **Double-spaced heading and paper**

7 November 2004

¶ indented 5 spaces or 1/2"   No, Thanks, I'll Pass on That   **Title centered**

1   One night at work my friend Kate turned down my offer of a red licorice stick after quickly checking the ingredients on the bag. I asked her to explain why, and she replied that they contained hydrogenated oils, which are, according to research articles she had read, "silent killers." She went on briefly to describe the horrors they do to your body, the various foods that contain them, as well as the effort she makes to avoid hydrogenated oils. I was shocked and intrigued by this news and decided to explore the reality of what she'd said.

2   A day or two later, while browsing through the shelves at the supermarket, I started checking ingredients. To my astonishment I couldn't seem to find a snack without these words on the back. Whether followed by the word "coconut," "cottonseed," or "soy bean," there it was lurking amidst the other ingredients-- hydrogenated oil. I was horrified! Thinking these scary oils couldn't be everywhere, I continued my search. A box of toaster tarts, again yes. A can of soup, there it was. I picked up a bag of pretzels, tossed it back on the shelf, and left the store in frustration, needless to say without buying a snack. Returning home I realized I needed to know the truth; I set out to find the answers to my questions.

3   My first question was this: what exactly does it mean to hydrogenate an oil? This is where things get a little technical: to hydrogenate is to add hydrogen. During the hydrogenation process the hydrogen atoms of a fatty acid are moved to the opposite side of the double bond of its molecular structure (Roberts). According to Lewis Harrison, author of <u>The Complete Fats and Oils Book</u>, this changed fatty acid molecule can actually be toxic to the body. It can cause oxidative stress and damage the body in the same way as cigarette smoke and chemical toxins. It can alter the normal transport of minerals and nutrients across cell membranes. As a result, foreign invaders may pass the cell membrane unchallenged; also supplies and information important to the cell may not be allowed in. Good fats that the body uses for many functions are not allowed to pass through the membrane while these fatty acids build up unused outside the cell, making us fat (Armstrong; Rudin and Felix 21).

4   To formulate hydrogenated oils, gas is fused into the oils using a metal catalyst (such as aluminum, cobalt, and nickel). These metals are needed to fuse the hydrogen into the oils. After hydrogenation these fatty acids are called trans-fatty acids or hydrogenated oils (Harrison 93). As a result, my licorice snacks were making me fat--which was a given--but not only that. They were actually disrupting the normal functions of my cells. What was this doing to me in the long run?

Paper continues, investigating research questions.

American Heart Association. "Hydrogenated Fats." 2002. 26 Oct. 2003

    <http://www.amhrt.org/presenter.jhtml?identifier=4662>.

Armstrong. Eric. "What's Wrong with Partially Hydrogenated Oils?" <u>Treelight</u>

    <u>Health.com.</u> 2001. 30 Sept. 2003 <http://www.treelight.com/health/

    PartiallyHydrogenatedOils.html>.

Harrison, Lewis. <u>The Complete Fat and Oils Book</u>. New York: Avery-Penguin, 1996.

Marshall, James R. "Trans Fatty Acids in Cancer." <u>Nutrition Reviews</u> May 1996.

Additional
lines
indented   Abstract. <u>Health and Wellness Resource Center</u>. Gale. U of Rhode Island

5 spaces
or ½''   Lib. 26 Oct. 2003 <http://galenet.galegroup.com>.

    Roberts, Shauna S. "IOM Takes Aims at Trans Fats." <u>Diabetes Forecast</u> 56

        (2003): 17-18. <u>Academic Search Premier</u>. EBSCO. U of Rhode Island Lib.

        26 Oct. 2003 <http://0-web20.epnet.com>.

Rudin, Donald, and Clara Felix. <u>The Omega-3 Phenomenon</u>. New York: Rawson

    Assoc., 1987.

"Think Before You Eat: Trans Fats Lurking in Many Popular Foods." <u>Knight</u>

    <u>Ridder/Tribune News Service</u> 8 Sept. 2003. <u>InfoTrac OneFile</u>. Providence

    Public Lib., RI. 26 Oct. 2003 <http://web4.infotrac.galegroup.com>.

United States Food and Drug Administration. "What Every Consumer Should

    Know About Trans Fatty Acids." 9 July 2003. 23 Oct. 2003 <http://

    www. fda.gov/oc/initiatives/transfat/q_a.html>.

GUIDE TO APA FORMATS

APA Formats for In-Text (Parenthetical) Citations

APA Formats for References

Books and Works Treated as Books

Articles from Periodicals and Selections from Books

Field and Media Resources

(continued)

14 | APA Style

The APA (American Psychological Association) documentation style uses the author's name and the date of publication—within parentheses or the text—to identify a source. This in-text citation guides readers to a detailed entry in a reference list at the end of the paper.

Use this "name-and-date" style when you write in a social science field or in a workplace or public setting where readers prefer a name-and-date system or want to see immediately how current your sources are.

For more information on APA style, consult the *Publication Manual of the American Psychological Association* (5th ed., Washington, DC: APA, 2001) or updates posted on the APA Web site: <http://www.apastyle.org>.

14a APA in-text (parenthetical) citations

In the APA system, you generally use parentheses in the text to enclose references to your sources, noting author and date, separated by a comma. You may also mention the author's name in your discussion instead of the citation.

1. Author's Name in Parentheses

IN PARENTHESIS   Teenagers who survive suicide attempts experience distinct

stages of recovery (Mauk & Weber, 1991).

2. Author's Name in Discussion

IN DISCUSSION   For Gitlin (2001), emotion is the basis of the connection

between fan and celebrity.

3. Specific Reference

To specify the location of a quotation, paraphrase, or summary, add a comma, *p.* or *pp.*, and then the page or pages in the source.

QUOTATION   One recent study examines the emotional intensity of "the

fan's link to the star" (Gitlin, 2001, p. 129).

For classical works, indicate the part you are citing (chap. 5), not the page. Spell any potentially confusing words and the word *figure*, but use *para.* or ¶ for a paragraph in an electronic source.

4. One Author

You can vary your in-text citations by presenting the name in the text, both the name and date in parentheses, or both in the text.

Dell's 2002 study of charter schools confirmed trends identified earlier

(James, 1996) and updated Rau's school classification (1998).

5. Two Authors

Include both names. Separate them with an ampersand (&) in parenthetical citations; in your text, use *and*.

Given evidence that married men earn more than unmarried men (Chun

& Lee, 2001), Nakosteen and Zimmer (2001) investigate how earnings

affect spousal selection.

6. Three to Five Authors

For the first citation, include all the names, separated by commas with *and* in the text or an ampersand (&) in parentheses.

Sadeh, Raviv, and Gruber (2000) related "sleep problems and

neuropsychological functioning in children" (p. 292).

In any subsequent references, use the first author's name with *et al.* ("and others"): Sadeh et al. (2000) reported their findings.

7. Six or More Authors

In text citations, follow the first author's name with *et al.* (Berg et al., 1998). (See Entry 2, p. 97.)

8. Corporate or Group Author

Spell out the name of the association, corporation, or government agency in the first citation. Follow any cumbersome name with an abbreviation in brackets so you can use the shorter form in later citations.

FIRST CITATION   Besides instilling fear, hate crimes limit where women live and

work (National Organization of Women [NOW], 2001).

LATER CITATION   Pending legislation would strengthen the statutes on

bias-motivated crimes (NOW, 2001).

9. No Author Given

Give the title or the first few words of a long title.

These photographs represent people from all walks of life (*Friendship*,

2001).

Full title: *Friendship: Celebration of humanity*.

10. Work Cited More Than Once

When you cite the same source more than once in a paragraph, repeat the citation as necessary to clarify a page reference or specify one of several sources. If a second reference is clear, don't repeat the date.

Much of the increase in personal debt can be linked to unrestrained

use of credit cards (Schor, 1998, p. 73). In fact, according to Schor,

roughly a third of consumers "describe themselves as either heavily or

moderately in financial debt" (p. 72).

11. Authors with the Same Name

Add initials to distinguish authors with the same last name.

Scholars have examined the development of African American culture

during slavery and reconstruction (E. Foner, 1988), including the role

of Frederick Douglass in this process (P. Foner, 1950).

12. Personal Communications, Including Interviews and Email

Cite letters, memos, interviews, email, telephone conversations, and similar sources using the person's name, the phrase *personal communication*, and the full date. Omit these sources from your reference list.

> According to J. M. Hostos, the state no longer funds services duplicated
>
> by county agencies (personal communication, October 7, 2003).

13. Two or More Sources in a Citation

If you sum up information from several sources, list them all in your citation. Arrange them alphabetically, then oldest to most recent for works by the same author. Separate the author entries with semicolons.

> Several studies have related job satisfaction and performance (Faire,
>
> 2002; Hall, 1996, 2001).

14. Two or More Works by the Same Author in the Same Year

If you use works published in the same year by the same author or author team, alphabetize the works and add letters after the year to distinguish them.

> Gould (1987a, p. 73) makes a similar point.

15. Content Footnote

You may use a content footnote to expand material. In the text add a superscript number, placed slightly above the related line of text. Number notes consecutively. On a separate page at the end, below the centered heading "Footnotes," present the notes in numerical order, as in the text. Begin each with its superscript number. Indent a half inch (five to seven spaces) for the initial line in each note, and double-space all notes.

TEXT   I tape-recorded and transcribed all interviews.[1]

NOTE   [1]Although background noise obscured some parts of the

tapes, these gaps did not substantially affect the material

studied.

14b APA reference list

Your list of sources enables readers to identify and consult the sources you have cited.

- Begin the list with the centered title "References" on a separate page at the end of your text but before appendixes or notes. (See p. 113 for a sample list.)
- List your sources alphabetically by author (or title if there is no author), then oldest to most recent for those by the same author.
- Do not indent the first line of each entry; indent the rest of the entry in paragraph style, a half inch or five to seven spaces.
- Double-space the entire list. Leave a single space after a period in an entry (except in abbreviations such as U.S.).

Books and Works Treated as Books

Include the following information for books, pamphlets, and similar sources: last name of each author followed by a comma and the *initials only* of the first and middle names; year of publication in parentheses; title (capitalizing only the first word, the first word of a subtitle, and any proper names); city of publication (with the country or the state's postal abbreviation, except for major cities); and publisher's name, with *Press* or *Books* but without words such as *Inc.* or *Publishers*.

1. One Author

Wilson, W. J. (1996). *When work disappears: The world of the new urban poor*. New York, Knopf.

2. Two or More Authors

List up to six authors; add *et al.* to indicate any others.

Biber, D., Conrad, S., & Reppen, R. (1998). *Corpus linguistics: Investigating language structure and use*. Cambridge, England: Cambridge University Press.

3. Corporate or Group Author

Treat the group as author. When author and publisher are the same, use *Author* after the place instead of repeating the name.

Amnesty International. (2001). *Annual report 2001* [Brochure]. London:

Author.

4. No Author Given

Boas anniversary volume: Anthropological papers written in honor of Franz

Boas. (1906). New York: Stechert.

5. More Than One Work by the Same Author

List works chronologically.

Aronowitz, S. (1993). *Roll over Beethoven: The return of cultural strife.*

Hanover, NH: Wesleyan University Press.

Aronowitz, S. (2000). *From the ashes of the old: American labor and*

America's future. New York: Basic Books.

6. More Than One Work by the Same Author in the Same Year

Gould, S. J. (1987a). *Time's arrow, time's cycle: Myth and metaphor in the*

discovery of geological time. Cambridge, MA: Harvard University Press.

Gould, S. J. (1987b). *An urchin in the storm: Essays about books and ideas.*

New York: Norton.

7. One or More Editors

Bowe, J., Bowe, M., & Streeter, S. C. (Eds.). (2001). *Gig: Americans talk*

about their jobs. New York: Three Rivers Press.

8. Translator

Bourdieu, P. (1990). *In other words: Essays towards a reflexive sociology*
(M. Adamson, Trans.). Stanford, CA: Stanford University Press.

9. Edition Following the First

Groth-Marnat, G. (1996). *Handbook of psychological assessment* (3rd ed.).
New York: Wiley.

10. Reprint

Butler, J. (1999). *Gender trouble.* New York: Routledge. (Original work
published 1990)

11. Multivolume Work

Strachey, J., Freud, A., Strachey, A., & Tyson, A. (Eds.). (1966-1974). *The*
standard edition of the complete psychological works of Sigmund Freud
(J. Strachey et al., Trans.) (Vols. 3-5). London: Hogarth Press and the
Institute of Psycho-Analysis.

12. Anthology or Collection of Articles

Appadurai, A. (Ed.). (2001). *Globalization.* Durham: Duke University Press.

13. Encyclopedia or Reference Work

Winn, P. (Ed.). (2001). *Dictionary of biological psychology.* London:
Routledge.

14. *Diagnostic and Statistical Manual of Mental Disorders*

After an initial full in-text citation for this widely cited manual, use these
abbreviations: *DSM-III* (1980), *DSM-III-R* (1987), *DSM-IV* (1994), or *DSM-IV-TR* (2000).

American Psychiatric Association. (1994). *Diagnostic and statistical manual of mental disorders* (4th ed.). Washington, DC: Author.

15. Dissertation (Unpublished)

Gomes, C. S. (2001). *Selection and treatment effects in managed care.* Unpublished doctoral dissertation, Boston University.

16. Government Document

Select Committee on Aging, Subcommittee on Human Services, House of Representatives. (1991). *Grandparents' rights: Preserving generational bonds* (Com. Rep. No. 102-833). Washington, DC: U.S. Government Printing Office.

17. Report

Dossey, J. A. (1988). *Mathematics: Are we measuring up?* (Report No. 17-M-02). Princeton, NJ: Educational Testing Service. (ERIC Document Reproduction Service No. ED300207)

Articles from Periodicals and Selections from Books

For an article, provide the following information: author's name (last name first); date (in parentheses); title (without quotation marks, capitalizing only the first word of the main title and any subtitle or proper names); journal title (in italics, capitalizing all main words), volume number (in italics), and page numbers.

18. Article in Journal Paginated by Volume

Klein, R. D. (2003). Audience reactions to local TV news. *American Behavioral Scientist, 46,* 1661-1672.

19. Article in Journal Paginated by Issue

Sadeh, A., Raviv, A., & Gruber, R. (2000). Sleep patterns and sleep
disruptions in school-age children. *Developmental Psychology, 36*(3),
291-301.

20. Special Issue of Journal

Balk, D. E. (Ed.). (1991). Death and adolescent bereavement [Special
issue]. *Journal of Adolescent Research, 6*(1).

21. Article in Weekly Magazine

Adler, J. (1995, July 31). The rise of the overclass. *Newsweek, 126,* 33-34,
39-40, 43, 45-46.

22. Article in Monthly Magazine

Dold, C. (1998, September). Needles and nerves. *Discover, 19,* 59-62.

23. Article with No Author Given

True tales of false memories. (1993, July/August). *Psychology Today, 26,*
11-12.

24. Article in Newspaper

Murtaugh, P. (1998, August 10). Finding a brand's real essence. *Advertising
Age,* p. 12.

25. Editorial or Letter to the Editor

Ellis, S. (2001, September 7). Adults are problem with youth sports [Letter
to the editor]. *USA Today,* p. 14A.

26. Interview (Published)

Although APA does not specify a form for published interviews, you may wish to employ the following form.

Dess, N. K. (2001). The new body-mind connection (John T. Cacioppo)

[Interview]. *Psychology Today, 34*(4), 30-31.

27. Review with Title

McMahon, R. J. (2000). The Pentagon's war, the media's war [Review of the

book *Reporting Vietnam: Media and military at war*]. *Reviews in

American History,* 28, 303-308.

28. Review Without Title

Verdery, K. (2002). [Review of the book. *The politics of gender after

socialism*]. *American Anthropologist,* 104, 354-355.

29. Article in Encyclopedia or Reference Work

Chernoff, H. (1978). Decision theory. In *International encyclopedia of

statistics* (Vol. 1, pp. 131-135). New York: Free Press.

30. Chapter in Edited Book or Selection in Anthology

Chisholm, J. S. (1999). Steps to an evolutionary ecology of mind. In A. L.

Hinton (Ed.), *Biocultural approaches to the emotions* (pp. 117-150).

Cambridge, England: Cambridge University Press.

31. Dissertation Abstract

Yamada, H. (1989). American and Japanese topic management strategies in

business conversations. *Dissertation Abstracts International, 50*(09), 2982B.

Field and Media Resources

32. Unpublished Raw Data

Briefly describe field data in brackets; end with *Unpublished raw data.*

> Hernandez, J. (2004). [Survey of attitudes on unemployment benefits].
>
>> Unpublished raw data.

33. Interview (Unpublished)

Cite an interview you have conducted only in the text. (See Entry 12, p. 95, and Entry 26, p. 102).

34. Personal Communications (Including Email)

Cite letters, email, phone calls, and other communications that cannot be consulted by your readers only in the text. (See Entry 12, p. 95.)

35. Paper Presented at a Meeting

> Nelson, J. S. (1993, August). *Political argument in political science: A*
>
>> *meditation on the disappointment of political theory.* Paper presented
>>
>> at the annual meeting of the American Political Science Association,
>>
>> Chicago.

36. Videotape or Film

> Musen, K. (Producer/Writer), & Zimbardo, P. (Writer). (1990). *Quiet rage:*
>
>> *The Stanford prison study* [Motion picture]. (Available from Insight
>>
>> Media, New York)

37. Television or Radio Program

> Siceloff, J. L. (Executive Producer). (2002). *Now with Bill Moyers*
>
>> [Television series]. New York: WNET.

38. Recording

Freeman, R. (1994). Porscha [Recorded by R. Freeman & The Rippingtons].
On *Sahara* [CD]. New York: GRP Records.

Online and Electronic Resources

39. Web Site

Brown, D. K. (1998, April 1). *The children's literature web guide.* Calgary:
Author. Retrieved August 23, 1998, from http://www.acs
.UCalgary.ca/~dkbrown/

40. Online Book or Document

If you can't find a publication date, use *n.d.* ("no date").

Frary, R. B. (n.d.). *A brief guide to questionnaire development.* Retrieved
August 8, 1998, from http://ericae.net/ft/tamu/upiques3.htm

41. Selection from Online Book or Document

Lasswell, H. D. (1971). Professional training. In *A pre-view of policy
sciences* (chap. 8). Retrieved May 4, 2002, from http://www
.policysciences.org/spsresources.htm

42. Online Journal Article

Sheridan, J., & McAuley, J. D. (1998). Rhythm as a cognitive skill:
Temporal processing deficits in autism. *Noetica, 3*(8). Retrieved
December 31, 1998, from http://www.cs.indiana.edu/Noetica/
OpenForumIssue8/McAuley.html

43. Online Article Identical to Print Version

If online and print articles are identical, you may use the print format but identify the online version you used.

Epstein, R. (2001). Physiologist Laura [Electronic version]. *Psychology*

Today, 34(4), 5.

If the online article differs in format or content, add your retrieval date with the URL.

44. Online Newsletter Article

Cashel, J. (2001, July 16). Top ten trends for online communities. *Online*

Community Report. Retrieved October 18, 2001, from http://

www.onlinecommunityreport.com/features/10/

45. Online Newspaper Article

Phillips, D. (1999, June 13). 21 days, 18 flights. *Washington Post Online.*

Retrieved June 13, 1999, from http://www.washingtonpost.com/

wp-srv/business/daily/june99/odyssey13.htm

46. Online Organization or Agency Document

Arizona Public Health Association. (n.d.). *Indigenous health section.*

Retrieved September 6, 2001, from http://www.geocities.com/

native_health_az/AzPHA.htm

47. Online Government Document

U.S. Department of Labor, Women's Bureau. (2001). *Women's jobs*

1964-1999: More than 30 years of progress. Retrieved September 7,

2001, from http://www.dol.gov/dol/wb/public/jobs6497.htm

48. Online Document from Academic Site

Cultural Studies Program. (n.d.). Retrieved September 9, 2001, from Drake

University, Cultural Studies Web site: http://www.multimedia

.drake.edu/cs/

49. Online Report

Amnesty International. (1998). *The death penalty in Texas: Lethal injustice*.

Retrieved September 7, 2001, from http://www.web.amnesty.org/

ai.nsf/index/AMR510101998

50. Online Report from Academic Site

Use "Available from" rather than "Retrieved from" if the URL will take your
reader to access information rather than the source itself.

Vandell, D. L., & Wolfe, B. (2000). *Child care quality: Does it matter and

does it need to be improved?* (Special Report No. 78). Available from

University of Wisconsin, Institute for Research on Poverty Web site:

http://www.ssc.wisc.edu/irp/sr/sr78.pdf

51. Online Abstract

National Bureau of Economic Research. (1998). Tax incentives for higher

education. *Tax Policy and the Economy, 12,* 49-81. Abstract retrieved

August 24, 1998, from http://www-mitpress.mit.edu/

journal-editor.tcl?ISSN=08928649

52. Online Database: Journal Article

Piko, B. (2001). Gender differences and similarities in adolescents' ways

of coping. *Psychological Record, 51*(2), 223-236. Retrieved August 31,

2001, from InfoTrac Expanded Academic database.

53. Online Database: Newspaper Article

Sappenfield, M. (2002, June 24). New laws curb teen sports drugs. *The*

Christian Science Monitor. Retrieved June 26, 2002, from America

Online: News Publications database.

54. Presentation from Virtual Conference

Brown, D. J., Stewart, D. S., & Wilson, J. R. (1995). *Ethical pathways to*

virtual learning. Paper presented at the Center on Disabilities 1995

virtual conference. Retrieved September 7, 2001, from

http://www.csun.edu/cod/95virt/0010.html

55. Email

Cite email only in your text. (See Entry 12, p. 95.)

56. Online Posting

Treat these as personal communications (see Entry 12, p. 95) unless they
are archived and accessible.

Lanbehn, K. (2001, May 9). Effective rural outreach. Message posted to

State Independent Living Council Discussion Newsgroup, archived at

http://www.acils.com/silc/

57. Computer Program

Begin with the name of an author who owns rights to a program or with its title (without italics).

Family Tree Maker (Version 9.0) [Computer software]. (2001). Fremont, CA:

Learning Company.

58. CD-ROM Database

Hall, Edward T. (1998). In *Current biography: 1940-1997*. Retrieved March 14,

1999, from Wilson database.

14c APA sample pages

The APA manual recommends beginning a research paper with a title page, using the format illustrated on the facing page. This student writer also included an abstract before the paper and the questionnaire for the study in the appendix following it.

Number title page and all others using short title   Body Esteem 1

Running head: BODY ESTEEM   **Abbreviate title (50 characters maximum) for running head**

Center title and all other lines

Body Esteem in Women and Men

Sharon Salamone

Supply name and institution

University of Rhode Island

Professor Robert Schwegler

Writing 233

Section 2

April 30, 2003

Supply course information and date if requested by your instructor

Begin on new page

Body Esteem 2

Do not
indent   Center heading   Abstract

Undergraduate students, male and female, were asked to complete a Body

Esteem Survey to report attitudes toward their bodies (body images).

Responses to the survey provided an answer to the question of whether the

men or the women had higher body esteem. The mean responses for women

and men indicated a higher level of body esteem among men with a statistically

significant difference in the means. Because the sample was limited to college

undergraduates and displayed little variety in ethnicity (predominantly

White), the findings of the study are limited. Prior research on ethnicity

and body image suggests that a more ethnically varied sample might

produce different results.

Double-
space
abstract
and
paper

Summarize
paper in
one ¶, no
more than
120 words

Besides the abstract, typical
sections in an APA paper are
Introduction, Method, Results,
and Discussion

Begin on new page

↑

Indent ¶s
consistently ¹/₂"
or 5 to 7 spaces

1" from top

↓

Body Esteem in Men and Women   Title centered

1   The concept of beauty has changed over the years in Western society,
especially for women. In past centuries the ideal was a voluptuous and curved
body; now it is a more angular and thin shape (Monteath & McCabe, 1997).
Lean, muscular bodies are currently held up as ideals for men, too. Based on
such ideals of physical appearance, people considered attractive may be
preferred as working partners, as dating partners, or as job candidates
(Lennon, Lillethun, & Buckland, 1999). Media images endorse particular
body ideals as well; for example, "media in Western countries have portrayed
a steadily thinning female body ideal" (Monteath & McCabe, 1997, p. 711).

1"
margin
on each
side

2   Most of us assume that women are quite concerned about their weight
and appearance--their body images--and that they often lack positive body
esteem, perhaps as a result of media images and other cultural influences
(Polivy & Herman, 1987; Rodin, Silberstein, & Striegel-Moore, 1984). But what
about men? Is their level of body esteem higher or lower than women's or
about the same? In this paper I report on a study I undertook with a group of
college undergraduates to compare the attitudes of men and women toward
their bodies. In particular, I wanted to determine whether or not the men had
a higher body esteem than the women had.

1" margin at
bottom

Body Esteem 4

Introduction   **Center subheading**

3   Thinness is prized in contemporary society, especially for women. In our culture, thinness, a statistical deviation, has become the norm, leading millions of women to believe their bodies are abnormal. Therefore, it is reasonable for women to be concerned about their appearance and compare themselves to others on the basis of what they believe to be the norm (Lennon et al., 1999).

4   Body image is basically made up of two important components: one's perception and one's attitude toward body image. Social factors can play a large role in determining both components (Monteath & McCabe, 1997). Given the cultural pressures on women to be thin, we might expect many women to have somewhat negative body images.

5   On the other hand, some researchers suggest that "men seem less obsessed with and disturbed by being or becoming fat: thus, the occurrence of pathogenic values related to eating and body size is extremely low among men" (Demarest & Allen, 2000, p. 465). Although there is some research, "the literature on body image perception in men is far more limited" than that on women (Pope et al., 2000, p. 1297). Possible reasons to suspect that men also suffer from distorted perceptions of body image have been evident in two recent studies. First, men with eating disorders believe that they are fatter than men of normal weight believe. Also, recent studies have shown that

Paper continues.

Begin on new page

Do not indent first line

References

Demarest, J., & Allen, R. (2000). Body image: Gender, ethnic, and age

    differences. *Journal of Social Psychology, 140,* 465-471.

Lennon, S. J., Lillethun, A., & Buckland, S. S. (1999). Attitudes toward social

    comparison as a function of self-esteem: Idealized appearance and body

    image. *Family & Consumer Sciences Research Journal, 27,* 379-405.

Monteath, S. A., & McCabe, M. P. (1997). The influence of societal factors on

    female body image. *Journal of Social Psychology, 137,* 708-727.

Polivy, J., & Herman, C. P. (1987). The diagnosis and treatment of abnormal

    eating. *Journal of Consulting and Clinical Psychology, 55,* 635-644.

Rodin, J., Silberstein, L., & Striegel-Moore, R. (1984). Women and weight: A

    normative discontent. In T. B. Sonderegger (Ed.), *Nebraska symposium on*

    motivation: Psychology and gender (pp. 267-307). Lincoln: University of

    Nebraska Press.

Rosen, J. C., & Gross, J. (1987). Prevalence of weight reducing and weight

    gaining in adolescent boys and girls. *Health Psychology, 6,* 131-147.

Pope, H. G., Bureau, B., DeCol, C., Gruber, A. J., Hudson, J. I., Jouvent, R.,

    & Mangweth, B. (2000). Body image perception among men in three

    countries. *American Journal of Psychiatry, 157,* 1297-1301.

Indent each following line as you indent a ¶

GUIDE TO CMS FORMATS

CMS Formats for Endnotes and Footnotes

CMS Formats for Bibliography Entries

15 | CMS Style

The CMS (*Chicago Manual of Style*) outlines a system for references using endnotes or footnotes. These notes are less compact than parenthetical references but allow detailed citations. They work well when readers won't need to consult each note and might be distracted by information in parentheses. Use the CMS style in academic settings in the arts and sciences, such as history, or when an instructor requests "Turabian," "Chicago," or a footnote or endnote style.

The CMS style shown here is one of two documentation systems outlined in *The Chicago Manual of Style* (15th edition, Chicago: University of Chicago Press, 2003), often simply called "Chicago." Its Web site at <http://www.press.uchicago.edu/Misc/Chicago/cmosfaq.html> answers many questions for writers and editors who routinely use CMS. This style is detailed for students in Kate L. Turabian's *A Manual for Writers of Term Papers, Theses, and Dissertations* (6th ed., rev. John Grossman and Alice Bennett, Chicago: University of Chicago Press, 1996), known as "Turabian."

15a CMS notes

To indicate a reference in your text, add a superscript number above the line. Number all your references consecutively. Provide the details about the source at the end of the paper (endnote) or at the bottom of the page (footnote). A typical note supplies the author's name in regular order, title, publication information (without "Inc." and "Co."), and page reference.

TEXT   Wideman describes his childhood neighborhood as being not simply

on "the wrong side of the tracks" but actually "under the tracks."[1]

NOTE   1. John Edgar Wideman, *Brothers and Keepers* (New York: Penguin Books, 1984), 39.

Endnotes are easy to prepare (and easy for readers to consult), though some word processors can position footnotes between the text and the bottom margin. Place endnotes at the end of your paper, after any appendix but before the bibliography, which alphabetically orders your sources. Because readers may skip notes, put the essentials in your text. Avoid excessive detail on points of interest to only a few readers.

Supply your endnotes on a separate page with the centered heading "Notes." For each note, indent the first line like a paragraph. Start with the number, typed on the line and followed by a period and a space. Do not indent the lines that follow. CMS suggests double-spacing all parts of your text, but Turabian suggests single-spaced notes. We advise double-spacing for ease of reading.

TEXT   Another potential source of misunderstanding comes from differences

in the ways orders are given by men (directly) and women

(indirectly, often as requests or questions).[2]

NOTE   2. Deborah Tannen, "How to Give Orders Like a Man," *New York Times Magazine*, 18 August 1994, 46. Tannen provides a balanced, detailed discussion of the ways men and women use language in *Talking from 9 to 5* (New York: William Morrow, 1994).

Books and Works Treated as Books

1. One Author

1. Bobby Bridger, *Buffalo Bill and Sitting Bull: Inventing the Wild West* (Austin: University of Texas Press, 2002), 297.

2. Two Authors

2. William H. Gerdts and Will South, *California Impressionism* (New York: Abbeville Press, 1998), 214.

3. Three Authors

3. Michael Wood, Bruce Cole, and Adelheid Gealt, *Art of the Western World* (New York: Summit Books, 1989), 206-10.

4. Four or More Authors

Follow the name of the first with *and others*. (Generally supply all the names in the bibliography entry. See Entry 4, p. 123.)

4. Anthony Slide and others, *The American Film Industry: A Historical Dictionary* (New York: Greenwood Press, 1986), 124.

5. No Author Given

5. *The Great Utopia* (New York: Guggenheim Museum, 1992), 661.

6. One Editor

6. Valantasis, Richard, ed., *Religions of Late Antiquity in Practice* (Princeton: Princeton University Press, 2000), 266.

7. Two or More Editors

7. Cris Mazza, Jeffrey DeShell, and Elisabeth Sheffield, eds., *Chick-Lit 2: No Chick Vics* (Normal, IL: Black Ice Books, 1996), 173-86.

8. Author, Editor, and Translator

8. Francis Bacon, *The New Organon,* ed. Lisa Jardine, trans. Michael Silverthorne (Cambridge: Cambridge University Press, 2000), 45.

9. Edition Following the First

9. Thomas E. Skidmore and Peter H. Smith, *Modern Latin America,* 5th ed. (New York: Oxford University Press, 2001), 243.

10. Reprint

10. Henri Frankfort and others, *The Intellectual Adventure of Ancient Man* (1946; repr. Chicago: University of Chicago Press, 1977), 202-4.

11. Multivolume Work

11. Sigmund Freud, *The Standard Edition of the Complete Psychological Works of Sigmund Freud,* trans. James Strachey (London: Hogarth Press, 1953), 11:180.

Articles from Periodicals and Selections from Books

12. Article in Journal Paginated by Volume

12. Lily Zubaidah Rahim, "The Road Less Traveled: Islamic Militancy in Southeast Asia," *Critical Asian Studies* 35 (2003): 224.

13. Article in Journal Paginated by Issue

13. Jose Pinera, "A Chilean Model for Russia," *Foreign Affairs* 79, no. 5 (2000): 62-73.

14. Article in Magazine

14. Joan W. Gandy, "Portrait of Natchez," *American Legacy*, Fall 2000, 51-52.

15. Article in Newspaper

15. Janny Scott, "A Bull Market for Grant, A Bear Market for Lee," *New York Times*, sec. A, September 30, 2000.

16. Chapter in Edited Book

16. John Matviko, "Television Satire and the Presidency: *The Case of Saturday Night Live*," in *Hollywood's White House: The American Presidency in Film and History*, ed. Peter C. Rollins and John E. O'Connor (Lexington: University of Kentucky Press, 2003), 341.

17. Selection in Anthology

17. W. E. B. Du Bois, "The Call of Kansas," in *W. E. B. Du Bois: A Reader*, ed. David Levering Lewis (New York: Henry Holt, 1995), 113.

Field and Media Resources

18. Interview (Unpublished)

18. LeJon Will, interview by author, May 22, 2003, transcript, Tempe, AZ.

19. Audio or Video Recording

19. *James Baldwin*, VHS, directed by Karen Thorsen (San Francisco: California Newsreel, 1990).

Online and Electronic Resources

20. Online Book

20. Sharon Marcus, *Apartment Stories: City and Home in Nineteenth-Century Paris and London* (Berkeley: University of California Press, 1999), http://ark.cdlib.org/ark:13030/ft0d5n99jz/ (accessed October 15, 2003).

21. Online Older Book

21. Charles Darwin, *On the Origin of Species by Means of Natural Selection, or the Preservation of Favoured Races in the Struggle for Life* (1859; Project Gutenberg, 1998), ftp://sailor.gutenberg.org/pub/gutenberg/etext98/otoos10.txt (accessed November 1, 2003).

22. Online Journal Article

22. Alfred Willis, "A Survey of Surviving Buildings of the Krotona Colony in Hollywood," *Architronic* 8, no. 1 (1999), http://architronic.saed.kent.edu/ (accessed September 29, 2000).

23. Online Magazine Article

23. Alexander Barnes Dryer, "Our Liberian Legacy," *The Atlantic Online,* July 30, 2003, http://www.theatlantic.com/unbound/flashbks/liberia.htm (accessed October 24, 2003).

24. Online Newspaper Article

24. Joshua Klein, "Scaring up a Good Movie," *Chicago Tribune Online Edition,* October 28, 2003, http://www.chicagotribune.com/ (accessed October 28, 2003).

25. Web Site

25. Smithsonian Center for Folklife and Cultural Heritage, "2002 Smithsonian Folklife Festival: The Silk Road," Smithsonian Institution, http://www.folklife.si.edu/CFCH/festival2002.htm (accessed October 27, 2003).

26. Online Posting

26. Justin M. Sanders, e-mail to alt.war.civil.usa, February 15, 2002, http://groups.google.com/groups?q=civil+war&hl= en&lr=&ie=UTF -8&selm=civil-war-usa/faq/part2_1013770939%40rtfm.mit.edu&rnum=1 (accessed October 21, 2003).

27. CD-ROM

27. Rose, Mark, ed., "Elements of Theater," *The Norton Shakespeare Workshop CD-ROM* (New York: Norton Publishing, 1997), CD-ROM, version 1.1.

Multiple Sources and Sources Cited in Prior Notes

28. Multiple Sources

28. See Greil Marcus, *Mystery Train: Images of America in Rock 'n Roll Music* (New York: E. P. Dutton, 1975), 119; and Susan Orlean, "All Mixed Up," *New Yorker*, 22 June 1992, 90.

29. Work Cited More Than Once

In your first reference, provide full information. Later, provide only the author's last name, short title, and page.

29. Pinera, "Chilean," 63.

30. Wood, Cole, and Gealt, *Art,* 207.

If two notes in a row refer to the same source, you may use the abbreviation *Ibid.* ("in the same place") for the second note. (Add a new page reference when the specific page is different.)

> 31. Tarr, "'A Man,'" 183.
>
> 32. Ibid.
>
> 33. Ibid., 186.

15b CMS bibliography

In addition to your notes, provide readers with an alphabetical list of your sources, titled "Selected Bibliography," "Works Cited," "References," or something similar. Place this list on a separate page at the end of your paper, and center the title two inches below the upper edge. Continue the page numbering used for the text. Although we show single-spaced entries below to save space, we recommend double-spacing so your bibliography is easy to read. (Consult your instructor.) Do not indent the first line, but indent each subsequent line one-half inch or five spaces. Alphabetize entries by the authors' last names or by the first word of the title (excluding *A, An,* and *The*) if the author is unknown.

Books and Works Treated as Books

1. One Author

Bridger, Bobby. *Buffalo Bill and Sitting Bull: Inventing the Wild West.*
    Austin: University of Texas Press, 2002.

2. Two Authors

Gerdts, William H., and Will South. *California Impressionism.*
    New York: Abbeville Press, 1998.

3. Three Authors

Wood, Michael, Bruce Cole, and Adelheid Gealt. *Art of the Western World*. New York: Summit Books, 1989.

4. Four or More Authors

Slide, Anthony, Val Almen Darez, Robert Gitt, and Susan Perez Prichard. *The American Film Industry: A Historical Dictionary*. New York: Greenwood Press, 1986.

5. No Author Given

The Great Utopia. New York: Guggenheim Museum, 1992.

6. One Editor

Valantasis, Richard, ed. *Religions of Late Antiquity in Practice*. Princeton: Princeton University Press, 2000.

7. Two or More Editors

Mazza, Cris, Jeffrey DeShell, and Elisabeth Sheffield, eds. *Chick-Lit 2: No Chick Vics*. Normal, IL: Black Ice Books, 1996.

8. Author, Editor, and Translator

Bacon, Francis. *The New Organon*. Edited by Lisa Jardine. Translated by Michael Silverthorne. Cambridge: Cambridge University Press, 2000.

9. Edition Following the First

Skidmore, Thomas E., and Peter H. Smith. *Modern Latin America*. 5th ed. New York: Oxford University Press, 2001.

10. Reprint

Frankfort, Henri, H. A. Frankfort, John A. Wilson, Thorkild Jacobsen, and William A. Irving. *The Intellectual Adventure of Ancient Man.* 1946. Reprint, Chicago: University of Chicago Press, 1977.

11. Multivolume Work

Freud, Sigmund. *The Standard Edition of the Complete Psychological Works of Sigmund Freud.* Translated by James Strachey. Vol. 11. London: Hogarth Press, 1953.

Articles from Periodicals and Selections from Books

12. Article in Journal Paginated by Volume

Rahim, Lily Zubaidah. "The Road Less Traveled: Islamic Militancy in Southeast Asia." *Critical Asian Studies* 35 (2003): 209-32.

13. Article in Journal Paginated by Issue

Pinera, Jose. "A Chilean Model for Russia." *Foreign Affairs* 79, no. 5 (2000): 62-73.

14. Article in Magazine

Gandy, Joan W. "Portrait of Natchez." *American Legacy,* Fall 2000, 51-52.

15. Article in Newspaper

Scott, Janny. "A Bull Market for Grant, A Bear Market for Lee." *New York Times,* September 30, 2000, sec. A.

16. Chapter in Edited Book

Matviko, John. "Television Satire and the Presidency: The Case of *Saturday Night Live.*" In *Hollywood's White House: The American Presidency in Film and History,* edited by Peter C. Rollins and John E. O'Connor, 341-60. Lexington: University of Kentucky Press, 2003.

17. Selection in Anthology

Du Bois, W. E. B. "The Call of Kansas." In *W. E. B. Du Bois: A Reader,* edited by David Levering Lewis, 101-21. New York: Henry Holt, 1995.

Field and Media Resources

18. Interview (Unpublished)

Generally treat this as a personal or informal communication, cited only in your notes. (See Entry 18, p. 119.)

19. Audio or Video Recording

James Baldwin. VHS. Directed by Karen Thorson. San Francisco: California Newsreel, 1990.

Online and Electronic Resources

20. Online Book

Marcus, Sharon. *Apartment Stories: City and Home in Nineteenth-Century Paris and London.* Berkeley: University of California Press, 1999. http://ark.cdlib.org/ark:13030/ft0d5n99jz/ (accessed October 15, 2003).

21. Online Older Book

Darwin, Charles. *On the Origin of Species by Means of Natural Selection, or the Preservation of Favoured Races in the Struggle for Life*. London: Down, Bromley, Kent, 1859; Project Gutenberg, 1998. ftp://sailor.gutenberg.org/pub/gutenberg/etext98/otoos10.txt (accessed November 1, 2003).

22. Online Journal Article

Willis, Alfred. "A Survey of Surviving Buildings of the Krotona Colony in Hollywood." *Architronic* 8, no. 1 (1999), http://architronic.saed. kent.edu/(accessed September 29, 2000).

23. Online Magazine Article

Dryer, Alexander Barnes. "Our Liberian Legacy." *The Atlantic Online,* July 30, 2003. http://www.theatlantic.com/unbound/flashbks/ liberia.htm (accessed October 24, 2003).

24. Online Newspaper Article

Klein, Joshua. "Scaring up a Good Movie." *Chicago Tribune Online Edition,* October 28, 2003. http://www.chicagotribune.com/ (accessed October 28, 2003).

25. Web Site

Smithsonian Center for Folklife and Cultural Heritage. "2002 Smithsonian Folklife Festival: The Silk Road." Smithsonian Institution. http://www.folklife.si.edu/CFCH/festival2002.htm (accessed October 27, 2003).

26. Online Posting

Treat this as a personal or informal communication, cited only in your notes. (See Entry 26, p. 121.)

27. CD-ROM

Rose, Mark, ed. "Elements of Theater." *The Norton Shakespeare Workshop CD-ROM*. CD-ROM, version 1.1. New York: Norton Publishing, 1997.

Multiple Sources

28. Multiple Sources

When a note mentions more than one source, list each one separately in your bibliography.

16 | CSE Style

One common form of documentation in the natural and applied sciences is the style used by CSE (Council of Science Editors), formerly CBE (Council of Biology Editors). This simplified international scientific style presents two options for documentation: a name-and-year and a number system.

Use CSE style when you write in scientific or technical fields or when your instructor requests "scientific documentation" or prefers a name-and-year or number system. Use it in engineering, too, modified to follow the style required in a particular journal or by your instructor. (See 16c.) CSE style tends to have more variations than other styles, mainly because different scientific fields have different requirements. Check expectations with your instructor, your readers, or the publication using the style you are following. For more information, see *Scientific Style and Format: The CBE Manual for Authors, Editors, and Publishers* (6th ed., Cambridge, Eng.: Cambridge University Press, 1994), or visit <http://www.councilscienceeditors.org>.

16a CSE in-text citations

With the **name-and-year method,** include the author's name and the publication date in parentheses (unless mentioned in the text).

NAMED IN PARENTHESES

Decreases in the use of lead, cadmium, and zinc have resulted in a "large decrease in the large-scale pollution of the troposphere" (Boutron and others 1991, p 64).

NAMED IN TEXT

Boutron and others (1991) found that decreases in the use of lead, cadmium, and zinc have resulted in a "large decrease in the large-scale pollution of the troposphere" (p 64).

Distinguish several works by the same author, all dated in a single year, by letters (*a, b, c*) after the date. Use *p* with no period before a page number.

With the **number method,** place numbers in parentheses in the text (1) or raised above the line[1,2]; list corresponding numbered works as references.

Decreased use of lead, cadmium, and zinc have reduced pollution (1).

Your first option is to number in-text citations in order as they appear and to arrange them accordingly in the reference list. Your second is to alphabetize your references first, number them, and then use that number in your paper, also noting any important author's name.

16b CSE reference list

You may use "References" or "Cited References" to head your list. For the name-and-year method, alphabetize sources by the last name of the main author, and then order works by the same author by date, oldest first. After the author's name, add the date and a period. For the consecutive number method, arrange sources in the same sequence in your references as in your paper. For the alphabetized number method, alphabetize the entries, and then number them. The examples below illustrate the number method.

Books and Works Treated as Books

1. One Author

End the entry with the total number of pages in a book.

> 1. Bishop RH. Modern control systems analysis and design using MATLAB. Reading: Addison-Wesley; 1993. 239 p.

2. Two or More Authors

> 2. Freeman JM, Kelly MT, Freeman JB. The epilepsy diet treatment: an introduction to the ketogenic diet. New York: Demo, 1994. 180 p.

3. Corporate or Group Author

3. Intergovernmental Panel on Climate Change. Climate change 1995: the science of climate change. Cambridge: Cambridge Univ Pr; 1996. 572 p.

4. Editor

4. Dolphin D, editor. Biomimetic chemistry. Washington: American Chemical Soc; 1980. 437 p.

5. Translator

5. Jacob F. The logic of life: a history of heredity. Spillmann BE, translator. New York: Pantheon Books; 1982. 348 p. Translation of: Logique du vivant.

6. Conference Proceedings

6. Witt I, editor. Protein C: biochemical and medical aspects. Proceedings of the International Workshop; 1984 Jul 9-11; Titisee, Germany. Berlin: De Gruyter; 1985. 195 p.

7. Report

7. Environmental Protection Agency (US) [EPA]. Guides to pollution prevention: the automotive repair industry. Washington: US EPA; 1991; 46 p. Available from: EPA Office of Research and Development; EPA/625/7-91/013.

Articles from Periodicals and Selections from Books

8. Article in Journal Paginated by Volume

8. Yousef YA, Yu LL. Potential contamination of groundwater from Cu, Pb, and Zn in wet detention ponds receiving highway runoff. J Environ Sci Health 1992;27:1033-44.

9. Article in Journal Paginated by Issue

9. Boutron CF. Decrease in anthropogenic lead, cadmium and zinc in Greenland snows since the late 1960's. Nature 1991;353(6340):153-5, 160.

10. Article with Corporate or Group Author

10. Derek Sims Associates. Why and how of acoustic testing. Environ Eng 1991;4(1):10-12.

11. Entire Issue of Journal

11. Savage A, editor. Proceedings of the workshop on the zoo-university connection: collaborative efforts in the conservation of endangered primates. Zoo Biol 1989;1(Suppl).

12. Chapter in Edited Book or Selection in Anthology

12. Moro M. Supply and conservation efforts for nonhuman primates. In: Gengozian N, Deinhardt F, editors. Marmosets in experimental medicine. Basel: S. Karger AG; 1978. p 37-40.

13. Figure from Article

13. Kanaori Y, Kawakami SI, Yairi K. Space-time distribution patterns of destructive earthquakes in the inner belt of central Japan. Eng Geol 1991;31(3-4):209-30 (p 210, table 1).

Online and Electronic Resources

CSE follows the National Library of Medicine online formats.

14. Patent from Database or Information Service

14. Collins FS, Drumm ML, Dawson DC, Wilkinson DJ, inventors. Method of testing potential cystic fibrosis treating compounds using cells in

culture. US patent 5,434,086. 1995 Jul 18. Available from:
Lexis/Nexis/Lexpat library/ALL file.

15. Online Article

15. Grolmusz V. On the weak mod m representation of Boolean functions.
Chi J Theor Comp Sci [Serial online] 1995; 100-5. Available from:
http://www.csuchicago.edu/publication/cjtcs/articles/1995/2/
contents.html. Accessed 1996 May 3.

16. Online Abstract

16. Smithies O, Maeda N. Gene targeting approaches to complex genetic
diseases: atherosclerosis and essential hypertension [abstract]. Proc
Natl Acad Sci USA [Serial online]. 1995; 92(12):5266-72. 1 screen.
Available from: Lexis/Medline/ABST. Accessed 1996 Jan 21.

16c Variations in scientific and technical style

CSE is a flexible style with widely accepted variations.

STRATEGY **Adapt CSE style to meet community expectations.**

- Review the general CSE guidelines and major alternative patterns.
- Follow any specific directions supplied by your instructor, advisor, or supervisor. Ask what's expected if you aren't sure how to proceed.
- Check any specific guidelines or style manuals in your specialized scientific, engineering, or technical field.
- Look for guidelines for authors in the front or back of a recommended or respected journal or on the sponsoring organization's Web site. Modify directions as necessary to fit your document.
- Match your own paper against any paper or journal article suggested as a pattern. Edit your in-text citations to follow the pattern in your model. Order the entries in your reference list as your model does. Arrange the details for each reference in the same way, checking punctuation, capitalization, italics, and so on.

PART
4
Writing Correctly

Voices
from the Community

"All I know about grammar is its infinite power. To shift the structure of a sentence alters the meanings of that sentence, as inflexibly as the position of a camera alters the meanings of the object photographed. . . . The arrangement of the words matters, and the arrangement you want can be found in the picture in your mind." Joan Didion, "Why I Write"

17 | Fragments

If you write a group of words that masquerades as a sentence but is incomplete, you may irritate or mislead your readers and undermine your own authority as a writer.

PARTS MISSING   The insurance company processing the claim.

        READER'S REACTION: Something is missing. What did it *do*?

EDITED   The insurance company processing the claim **sent** a check.

Even with a capital letter at the beginning and a period at the end, a **sentence fragment** is only part of a sentence—it may lack a **subject** (naming the doer) or a **verb** (naming the action or occurrence). It may be a **subordinate clause,** introduced by a word like *because* and mistakenly asked to stand on its own.

 17a Recognizing sentence fragments

Subject and verb. A **complete sentence** must contain both a subject and a complete verb, expressed or implied.

> **STRATEGY** Ask questions to identify fragments and sentences.
>
> • Test #1: Ask *who* or *what does*? Or *Who* or *what is*?
>
> A word group that doesn't answer "Who?" or "What?" lacks a subject and is a fragment. Especially if it begins with *and* or *but,* it may be detached from a nearby sentence with its subject.
>
> **FRAGMENT**   And also needs a counselor.
>
>   **READER'S REACTION: I can't tell *who* (or *what*) needs the counselor.**
>
> **EDITED**   **Hope Clinic hired a nurse** and also needs a counselor.

A word group that doesn't answer "Does?" or "Is?" lacks a complete verb and is a fragment.

FRAGMENT   The new policy to provide coverage on the basis of hours worked.

> **READER'S REACTION: I can't tell what the policy *does* or *is*.**

EDITED   The new policy **provides** coverage on the basis of hours worked.

- Test #2: Can you turn a word group into a question that can be answered *yes* or *no*? If you can, it's a sentence.

Caution: Begin your question with *did*. If you begin with *is, are, has,* or *have,* you may provide a missing verb.

WORD GROUPS   They signed the petition to recall the mayor. Suspecting his involvement.

QUESTIONS   Did they sign the petition to recall the mayor? [Yes.] Did suspecting his involvement? [Can't answer.]

CONCLUSION   The first word group is a sentence, but not the second.

Subordinating words. Look for a **clause** (a word group with a subject and verb) introduced by a subordinating conjunction (*although, if, because, unless;* see 27b) or a pronoun (*that, what, which, who*). If this word group is not attached to a main clause that can stand alone, it's a fragment.

STRATEGY Hunt for a subordinating word.

FRAGMENT   Residents love the mild climate. Which is ideal for outdoor events.

EDITED   Residents love the mild climate**,** which is ideal for outdoor events.

SERIOUS ERROR

17b Editing sentence fragments

Complete or attach fragments so that you supply what's missing.

STRATEGY Attach, rewrite, add, or omit.

- Attach a fragment to a nearby sentence.

  FRAGMENT Trauma centers give prompt care to heart attack victims. Because **rapid treatment can minimize heart damage.**

  ATTACHED Trauma centers give prompt care to heart attack victims **because** rapid treatment can minimize heart damage.

- Rewrite to eliminate the fragment.

  FRAGMENT **Introducing competing varieties of crabs into the same tank.** He did this in order to study aggression.

  REWRITTEN He **introduced** competing varieties of crabs into the same tank in order to study aggression.

- Drop a subordinating word.

  FRAGMENT Although **the advisory committee contested the motion.** It still passed by a majority.

  EDITED The advisory committee contested the motion. It still passed by a majority.

- Supply a missing word.

  FRAGMENT **The judge allowing adopted children to meet their natural parents.**

  EDITED The judge **favors** allowing adopted children to meet their natural parents.

17c Using partial sentences

Especially in advertising and creative writing, you'll see *deliberate* fragments used for emphasis or contrast. Use such fragments only when readers will recognize your intention and accept the resulting style. In most academic and professional writing, avoid them.

18 | Comma Splices and Fused Sentences

You may confuse or annoy readers if you inappropriately join two or more sentences using either a comma (**comma splice**) or no punctuation at all (**fused sentence**).

COMMA SPLICE
CBS was founded in 1928 by William S. Paley, his uncle and his father sold him a struggling radio network.

READER'S REACTION: At first I thought that CBS had three founders: Paley, his uncle, and his father.

EDITED
CBS was founded in 1928 by William S. Paley**;** his uncle and his father sold him a struggling radio network.

FUSED SENTENCE
The city had only one swimming pool without an admission fee the pool was in disrepair.

READER'S REACTION: Is there only one pool, or is there only one that's free?

EDITED
The city had only one swimming pool**, but** without an admission fee, the pool was in disrepair.

A **comma splice** links what could be two sentences with a comma alone. A **fused** (or **run-on**) sentence joins what could be two sentences without any punctuation mark or connecting word at all. Either can confuse a reader about where one part ends and another begins.

18a Recognizing comma splices

Look for sentences with word groups that could stand on their own but are joined by a comma.

<table>
<tr><td colspan="2">**STRATEGY** | Hunt for commas that string word groups together.</td></tr>
</table>

| **COMMA SPLICE** | The typical Navajo husband is a trustee, the wife and her children own the property. |
| **EDITED** | The typical Navajo husband is a trustee **, but** the wife and her children own the property. |

READER'S REACTION: Until you added *but,* I missed your point about the wife's status.

18b Recognizing fused sentences

Though fused sentences may be any length, look for long sentences with little or no internal punctuation.

STRATEGY | Count the statements in a sentence.

If you find several, check the punctuation and connecting words.

| **FUSED SENTENCE** | The scientists had trouble identifying the fossil it resembled a bird and a lizard. |
| **EDITED** | The scientists had trouble identifying the fossil **because** it resembled a bird and a lizard. |

READER'S REACTION: Adding *because* separates the two main points and clarifies the sentence.

18c Editing comma splices and fused sentences

As you repair sentences, decide how to relate or connect ideas.

STRATEGY | Separate or relate ideas for emphasis.

• Divide into two sentences.
  (_____. _____.)

| **FUSED SENTENCE** | Football does not cause the most injuries in college gymnastics is more dangerous. |

EDITED   Football does not cause the most injuries in college. **G**ymnastics is more dangerous.

- Join with a comma plus *and, but, or, for, nor, so,* or *yet.*
(_____, and _____.)

FUSED SENTENCE   The clinic is understaffed it still performs well.

EDITED   The clinic is understaffed **, yet** it still performs well.

- Connect similar or equal ideas with a semicolon.
(_____; _____.)

COMMA SPLICE   An autopilot corrects drift, the system senses and reacts to changes in the aircraft's motion.

EDITED   An autopilot corrects drift **;** the system senses and reacts to changes in the aircraft's motion.

- Make one part subordinate to relate ideas.
(Because _____, _____.)

A subordinator (*because, though, when, unless*) or relative pronoun (*who, which, that*) can show how one idea depends on another (see 27b).

COMMA SPLICE   Automobiles are so complex, mechanics may train for years.

EDITED   **Because** automobiles are so complex **,** mechanics may train for years.

- Clarify how parts relate with words and a semicolon.
(_____; therefore, _____.)

Use words like *however* and *moreover* (conjunctive adverbs, see 27a) or *for example, consequently,* or *in contrast* plus a semicolon.

FUSED SENTENCE   Chickens reach market size within months the lobster takes six to eight years.

EDITED   Chickens reach market size within months **; in contrast,** the lobster takes six to eight years.

ESL ADVICE: Similar Connecting Words

Some connecting words may mean the same thing but need different punctuation. The most common pair is *but* and *however*.

Jose likes his job **,** **but** the hours are long.

Jose likes his job **;** **however** **,** the hours are long.

Because introduces a clause with a subject and verb; *because of* introduces a prepositional phrase.

Because the pay is low, Anna wants a new job.

Because of the low pay, Anna wants a new job.

19 | Pronoun Reference

When you replace nouns with pronouns, you reduce repetition as you build connections. If readers can't tell which word is replaced, they may be irritated trying to figure out what your sentence means.

AMBIGUOUS
REFERENCE

In the circus, Brad's chores included leading the elephants from the cages and hosing **them** down.

READER'S REACTION: **What got hosed down? Elephants? Cages? Both?**

EDITED

In the circus, Brad's chores included hosing the elephants down after leading **them** from **their** cages.

Most problems occur when an **antecedent**—the word or words to which the pronoun refers—isn't clear. By creating clear pronoun reference, you tie ideas together, clarify relationships, and focus readers' attention.

19a Recognizing unclear pronoun reference

If readers say they "can't figure out what you're saying," make sure that each pronoun refers clearly to only one possible antecedent that is stated specifically and located close enough to make the connection clear.

> **STRATEGY** Mark a clear antecedent for each pronoun.

- Can you underline a *single, clear* antecedent?

   AMBIGUOUS REFERENCE   Robespierre disagreed with Danton over the path the French Revolution should take. **He** believed that the Revolution was endangered by internal enemies.

   READER'S REACTION: I'm lost. Who's *he*? Robespierre or Danton?

   EDITED   Robespierre disagreed with Danton over the path the French Revolution should take. **Robespierre** believed that the Revolution was endangered by internal enemies.

- Can you answer, "What does [pronoun X] refer to?"

   IMPLIED ANTECEDENT   A hard frost damaged local citrus groves, but **it** has not been determined

   READER'S REACTION: What does *it* mean—the frost? The damage? Or something else?

   STATED   A hard frost damaged local citrus groves, but **the extent of the loss** has not been determined.

19b Editing pronoun reference

Focus on the pronoun. If needed, clarify the antecedent or rewrite.

> **STRATEGY** Specify or explain the pronoun.

- Replace the pronoun with the noun to which it refers or with a synonym, or reword.

AMBIGUOUS
REFERENCE
Detaching the measuring probe from the glass cylinder is a delicate job because **it** breaks easily.

READER'S REACTION: Which is so fragile, the probe or the cylinder?

REPLACED
WITH NOUN
Detaching the measuring probe from the glass cylinder is a delicate job because **the probe** breaks easily.

REWORDED
Because the measuring probe breaks easily, detaching it from the glass cylinder is a delicate job.

• Right after *which, this,* or *that,* specify or explain the word to which the pronoun refers.

VAGUE
REFERENCE
Redfish have suffered from oil pollution and the destruction of their swamp habitat. **This** has reduced the redfish population.

READER'S REACTION: Does *this* refer to the destruction of habitat, the pollution, or both?

SPECIFIED
Redfish have suffered from oil pollution and the destruction of their swamp habitat. **This combination** has reduced the redfish population.

Sometimes a pronoun doesn't have to be replaced, just moved—especially to place *who, which,* and *that* right after their antecedents.

STRATEGY   **Move the pronoun close to its antecedent.**

CONFUSING
After our dog died, I found an old ball behind **a bush that he loved to chase.**

EDITED
After our dog died, I found behind a bush an **old ball that he loved to chase.**

Especially for many academic readers, a possessive noun used as an antecedent will appear to be an error.

STRATEGY	**Eliminate the possessive, and rewrite.**
INAPPROPRIATE	In Faulkner's *The Sound and the Fury,* **he** begins from the point of view of a mentally retarded person.
EDITED	In *The Sound and the Fury*, **Faulkner** begins from the point of view of a mentally retarded person.

Remedy problems and guide readers by creating a **reference chain** of pronouns whose antecedent is stated in the first sentence of a passage.

UNCLEAR	Sand paintings were a remarkable form of Pueblo art. An artist would sprinkle dried sand of different colors, ground flower petals, corn pollen, and similar materials onto the floor to create **them.** Encouraging the spirits to send good fortune to humans was **their** purpose.

Because *them* and *their* are buried at the ends of sentences in the middle of the paragraph, readers may lose sight of the topic: sand paintings.

EDITED TO CREATE A REFERENCE CHAIN	Sand paintings were a remarkable form of Pueblo art. To create **them,** the artist would sprinkle dried sand of different colors, ground flower petals, corn pollen, and similar materials onto the floor. **Their** purpose was to encourage the spirits to send good fortune to humans.

STRATEGY Create a reference chain.

- State the antecedent clearly in the opening sentence.
- Let no other possible antecedents interrupt the chain's links.
- Don't interrupt the chain and try to return to it later.
- Place the pronouns prominently (usually beginning sentences); vary their positions only slightly.

20 | Agreement

You give readers mixed signals if you don't coordinate sentence parts.

INCONSISTENT   The city council and the mayor is known for her skillful responses to civic debate.

> **READER'S REACTION: This sentence opens with two things—the city council and the mayor—but *is* and *her* seem to switch to only the mayor.**

EDITED   The city council and the mayor **are** known for **their** skillful responses to civic debate.

Readers expect to see how ideas in a sentence relate to each other grammatically—by showing **agreement** in number, person, and gender.

 20a Recognizing agreement

A subject and verb in a sentence should agree in number and person. A pronoun (*I, you, she*) should agree with its **antecedent,** the noun or other pronoun to which it refers, in number, person, and gender.

AGREEMENT: NUMBER, PERSON, GENDER

- **Number** shows singular (one) or plural (two or more) items.
  This **community** needs its recreation center.
  These **communities** need to share their facilities.

- **Person** indicates the speaker or subject spoken to or about.
  FIRST PERSON (SPEAKER)   I, we
  SECOND PERSON (SPOKEN TO)   You, you
  THIRD PERSON (SPOKEN ABOUT) He, she, it, they

- **Gender** refers to masculine (*he, him*), feminine (*she, her*), or neuter (*it*) qualities attributed to a noun or pronoun.

20b Editing subject-verb agreement

Subjects and verbs should match, both singular or both plural.

STRATEGY Check the *-s* and *-es* endings.

Add -s or -es to make nouns plural but present tense verbs singular.

SINGULAR   The dam prevent**s** flooding. [third person]
PLURAL   The dam**s** prevent flooding.

Exceptions

- **Nouns with irregular plurals** (*person/people, child/children*) or with the same form for singular and plural (*moose/moose*)
- **Verbs with irregular forms**, including *be* and *have*

More complicated sentences may lead you to use the wrong verb form.

STRATEGY Find the *real* subject, and match the verb.

- Mark the subject (not nouns in other word groups). Decide whether it's singular or plural. Edit the verb (or change the subject) to agree.

    DRAFT   The use of new testing **techniques** have increased.
    REAL SUBJECT The <u>use</u> of new testing **techniques** have increased.
    EDITED   The **use** of new testing techniques **has increased**.

- Imagine the core sentence without any intervening expressions. Make the central noun and verb agree.

    DRAFT   A regular tune-up, along with frequent oil changes, pro-
                        long the life of your car.
                        IMAGINE: A regular tune-up, ~~along with frequent oil changes,~~ **prolong** the life of your car.

    EDITED   A regular tune-up, along with frequent oil changes, prolongs the life of your car.

ESL ADVICE: Separated Subjects and Verbs

Check for agreement if the subject and verb are separated.

PHRASE   A person **with sensitive eyes** has to wear sunglasses.

CLAUSE   A person **whose eyes are sensitive** has to wear sunglasses.

When the subject is the same in both clauses, the verbs must agree.

SAME SUBJECT   A person who wants to protect her eyes wears sunglasses.

Deciding whether some nouns are singular or plural can be tricky.

STRATEGY Use a pronoun to test your verb choice.

Decide which pronoun accurately represents a complicated subject: *he, she,* or *it* (singular) or *they* (plural). Read your sentence aloud using this replacement pronoun; edit the verb to agree.

DRAFT   The **news** about the job market [sounds? sound?] good.
                    PRONOUN TEST: I could replace "The news" with "it" and say "It sounds."

EDITED   The **news** about the job market **sounds** good.

TRICKY SINGULAR AND PLURAL NOUNS

* **Collective noun** naming a unit composed of more than one individual or thing: *staff, flock, audience, tribe*

  SINGULAR   The staff is hardworking. [group as a unit = *it*]
  PLURAL   The staff are caring people. [individual members = *they*]

* Titles of books or names of companies with plural nouns

  SINGULAR   *Hard Times* is a great novel.
  SINGULAR   Burgers to Go is profitable.

- Nouns with plural forms and singular meanings: *politics, mumps*
  SINGULAR   Economics is a popular field of study.

- Compound subjects joined by *and: the men and women*
  PLURAL   Ham and eggs are the main ingredients. [two units]
  SINGULAR   Ham and eggs is my favorite meal. [rarely one unit]

- Alternative subjects joined by *or (nor): the servers or the cook*
  The verb agrees with the *closer* noun.

    The auditor or the **accountants** review the statement.

    The accountants or the **auditor** reviews the statement.

- Subjects renamed after linking verbs (*is, seems, appears*)
  The verb agrees with the subject (not the words renaming it).

    The chief **obstacle** to change is the mayor and her allies.

Indefinite pronouns do not refer to specific ideas, people, or things. Most (*anyone, each*) require singular verbs, but a few (*both, few*) need plural verbs. Some (*all, most, some*) may take either verb form—singular to refer to something that cannot be counted or plural to refer to two or more items of something that can be counted.

SINGULAR   **All** of the food **is** gone.
                   food = food in general (not countable)
PLURAL   **All** of the supplies **are** gone.
                   supplies = many kinds (countable)

ESL ADVICE: Quantifiers

Quantifiers (*each, one, many*) show the amount or quantity of a noun.

EXPRESSIONS FOLLOWED BY PLURAL NOUN + SINGULAR VERB
Each of/Every one of/One of/None of   the **students** lives on campus.

EXPRESSIONS FOLLOWED BY PLURAL NOUN + PLURAL VERB
Several of/Many of/Both of   the **students** live off campus.

EXPRESSIONS FOLLOWED BY A SINGULAR OR A PLURAL VERB

Some of/Most of/All of/A lot of

> noncount noun + singular verb
> the **produce** <u>is</u> fresh.

Some of/Most of/All of/A lot of

> plural noun + plural verb
> the **vegetables** <u>are</u> fresh.

MUCH **AND** *MOST* **(WITHOUT** *OF***)**

NONCOUNT NOUN   **Much traffic** <u>occurs</u> during rush hour.

PLURAL NOUN   **Most Americans** <u>live</u> in or near cities.

TRICKY SINGULAR AND PLURAL PRONOUNS

- *Who, which,* and *that* as subjects of clauses

  Match the verb and the word to which the pronoun refers.

  He likes <u>a film</u> that <u>builds</u> suspense but <u>novels</u> that <u>show</u> character.
- *Each* or *every* before a compound subject

  SINGULAR   Each clerk and manager <u>checks</u> the log.
- *Each* and *every* after a compound subject

  PLURAL   The clerks and managers each <u>check</u> the log.

20c Editing pronoun-antecedent agreement

Work with either the pronoun or its **antecedent,** the word to which it refers. Edit to bring the other into agreement.

STRATEGY	**Mark the specific word to which a pronoun refers.**

INCONSISTENT   **Each** of the samples travels in their own case.

CLEAR   **Each** of the samples travels in its own case.

When indefinite pronouns (see p. 147) are singular, so are other pronouns that refer to them.

Somebody on the team left her racket on the court.

Each of the men has his own equipment.

To avoid sexist language, use plural pronouns and antecedents.

SEXIST	**Everybody** used charts in **his** sales **talk.**
INFORMAL (SPOKEN)	**Everybody** used charts in **their** sales **talks.**
WRITTEN	**All presenters** used charts in **their** sales **talks.**

ESL ADVICE: *This, That, These, Those*

To modify nouns, *this* and *that* are singular; *these* and *those* are plural.

INCONSISTENT	This crystals make snowflakes.
PLURAL	**These crystals** make snowflakes.
INCONSISTENT	Those experiment takes two days.
SINGULAR	**That experiment** takes two days.

21 | Correct Forms

If you misuse word forms, readers may doubt your ability as a writer and pay more attention to the error than to your point.

DRAFT	By Friday, him and me will submit the report.
	READER'S REACTION: *Him and me* **sounds uneducated. Who hired this person?**
EDITED	By Friday, **he and I** will submit the report.

Most readers expect you to edit your writing to use widely accepted forms of verbs, pronouns, adjectives, and adverbs.

21a Recognizing and editing verb forms

Verbs vary in **tense** as they show past, present, and future time.

Past tense -*ed* ending for regular verbs.   Be sure to write this ending even if you don't hear it pronounced before a -*d* or -*t* sound.

DRAFT	The company **use** to provide dental benefits.
EDITED	The company **used** to provide dental benefits.

Past tense irregular verbs.   Irregular verbs form the past tense in some way other than adding -*ed* (*run/ran*). (For a list, see p. 229.)

DRAFT	The movie characters **sweared** constantly.
EDITED	The movie characters **swore** constantly.

Verb forms in complex tenses.   Complex tenses (see p. 226) have a main verb and a helping verb. The main verb is a **participle, past** (-*ed*, -*en*, or irregular form) or **present** (-*ing* form). The **helping verb** is a form of *be*, *do*, or *have* or a verb such as *will* or *would*.

	helping verb + main verb (present participle)
-ING FORM	He <u>was</u> **loading** the delivery van.
	helping verb + main verb (past participle)
REGULAR VERB	Mike <u>has</u> **analyzed** the problem.
IRREGULAR VERB	Lynn <u>has</u> **brought** the equipment.

ESL ADVICE: Common Helping Verbs

Be: *am, is, are, was, were, be, being, been*
Have: *have, has, had*
Do: *do, does, did*
Modals: *could, should, would, ought to, can, may, might, must, shall, will*

Helping verbs in progressive tenses.   These past, present, and future forms show an action in progress using an -*ing* main verb: *is turning, was* *turning, will be turning.* (See the chart on p. 226.) In writing, use all the parts of the correct verb even if your spoken dialect omits them.

WORD OMITTED	The interview **starting** now.
EDITED	The interview **is starting** now.
WRONG FORM	The workers **was running** for the door.
EDITED	The workers **were running** for the door.

Past participles in perfect tenses. The present, past, and future perfect tenses combine a helping verb with the past participle (the *-ed, -en,* or irregular form) to show the order of events. (See the chart on p. 226.) Don't substitute the simple past tense for the past participle.

MISTAKEN PAST	Pete **had rode** for a year before his injury.
EDITED	Pete **had ridden** for a year before his injury.

Mood. Sentences can be classified by **mood,** the form of the verb that reflects the writer's or speaker's attitude.

- **Indicative:** statements intended as truthful or factual

  Motorcycle helmets **have reduced** injuries.

- **Imperative:** statements acting as commands

  Get a helmet.

- **Subjunctive:** statements expressing uncertainty—a supposition, prediction, possibility, desire, or wish

  If you **were** to crash, the helmet would protect your head.

  Jim's insurance requires that he **wear** a helmet.

The subjunctive appears in formal writing, often in **conditional statements** beginning with *if* and in *that* clauses with verbs such as *ask* or *request.* With *that,* use the basic present form (*wear, be*), even with the third person singular. With *if,* use the basic present, the past (*wore, were* not *was*), or the past perfect (*had worn* not *would have worn, had been*).

ESL ADVICE: Conditional Statements

Conditional statements depend on a condition or are imagined. Each type has an *if* clause and a result clause that combine different verb tenses.

Type I: True in the present

- Generally true in the present as a habit or as a fact

  if + subject + <u>present tense</u>   subject + <u>present tense</u>

  If **I** <u>drive</u> to school every day,   **I** <u>get</u> to class on time.

- True in the future as a one-time event

  if + subject + <u>present tense</u>   subject + <u>future tense</u>

  If **I** <u>drive</u> to school today,   **I** <u>will get</u> to class on time.

- Possibly true in the future as a one-time event

  if + subject + <u>present tense</u>   subject + <u>modal + base form verb</u>

  If **I** <u>drive</u> to school today,   **I** <u>may get</u> to class on time.

Type II: Untrue or contrary to fact in the present

if + subject + <u>past tense</u>   subject + <u>*would/could/might* + base form verb</u>

If **I** <u>drove</u> to school,   **I** <u>would arrive</u> on time.

For Type II, the form of *be* in the *if* clause is always *were*.

Type III: Untrue or contrary to fact in the past

  subject + <u>*would/could/might* +</u>
if + subject + <u>past perfect tense</u>   <u>*have* + past participle</u>

If **I** <u>had driven</u> to school,   **I** <u>would</u> not <u>have been</u> late.

Lie, lay, sit, set. These forms are confusing for many writers.

VERB	PRESENT	PAST	PAST PARTICIPLE
lie (oneself)	lie	lay	lain
lay (an object)	lay	laid	laid
sit (oneself)	sit	sat	sat
set (an object)	set	set	set

DRAFT	I **laid** down yesterday for a nap. I **have laid** down every afternoon for a week.
EDITED	I **lay** down yesterday for a nap. I **have lain** down every afternoon for a week.
DRAFT	Erica and Steve **sat** the projector on the table.
EDITED	Erica and Steve **set** the projector on the table.

21b Editing for clear tense sequence

Readers expect you to use one tense or to follow a logical sequence.

STRATEGY	Change tense to relate events in time.
LOGICAL	People **forget** that four candidates **ran** in 1948.
LOGICAL	The accountant **destroyed** the file because **no one had asked** him to save it.
LOGICAL	No one **had recognized** that food from cans sealed with lead solder **is** poisonous.

21c Recognizing pronoun forms

Pronouns change form to fit their roles in a sentence (see p. 230–231).

SUBJECT	I, you, he, she, it; we, you, they
	I ran out of leaflets, but **he** had plenty.
OBJECT	me, you, him, her, it; us, you, them
	Jamie gave **me** some extras for **them.**
POSSESSIVE	my, mine, your, yours, his, her, hers, its; our, ours, your, yours, their, theirs
	Our client chose **my** leaflet design, not **hers.**

Subject complement. A pronoun that renames the subject (a **subject complement**) follows *be* (*is, are, was, were*), using the subjective form.

     subject   subject complement
 The people assigned the report <u>were</u> **Trinh and I.**

STRATEGY Test for pronouns that rename the subject.

Reverse the sentence to make the pronoun the subject.

DRAFT	**The last art majors** to get jobs were Becky and **me.**
REVERSED	Becky and **me** were the last art majors to get jobs.
REVERSE TEST	**Me** was the last art major. [doesn't fit]
EDITED	The last art majors to get jobs were Becky and **I.**

Possessive pronouns. You may be tempted to add an 's to a possessive pronoun just as you do with a noun (**John's** car, the **cat's meow**).

STRATEGY Test your possessive pronouns.

Spell out *it's* as the expression it stands for: *it + is.* If the expansion fits, keep the apostrophe. If not, omit it.

DRAFT	The food pantry gave away all **it's** tuna.
TEST	The food pantry gave away all **it is** tuna.
EDITED	The food pantry gave away all **its** tuna.

21d Editing pronoun forms

Compound subjects and objects. Use the same form for a pronoun in a compound that you would use if it were by itself.

STRATEGY Try focus-imagine-choose.

- **Focus** on the questionable pronoun.

DRAFT	Anna and **me** will develop the video.
	FOCUS: *I* or *me*?

- **Imagine** each choice for the pronoun.

Me will develop the video. (no)

I will develop the video. (yes)

- **Choose** the correct form for the compound.

  EDITED   Anna and **I** will develop the video.

Appositives. When you rename a preceding noun or pronoun in an **appositive,** match the pronoun to the form of the word being renamed.

STRATEGY	Test possible replacements.
DRAFT	The two illustrators on the panel, **her** and **me,** answered questions.
REPLACEMENT	**Her** and **me** answered questions. (no)
REPLACEMENT	**She** and **I** answered questions. (yes)
EDITED	The two illustrators on the panel, **she and I,** answered questions.

Comparisons with *than* or *as*. When you end a comparison with a pronoun, choose the form based on the information left out.

| SUBJECT | I gave her sister more help than **she** [did]. |
| OBJECT | I gave her sister more help than [I gave] **her.** |

***Who* and *whom*.** Choose *who* and *whoever* as subjects; choose *whom* and *whomever* as objects. When the pronoun is in a clause, make your choice based on its role within the clause, not the sentence as a whole.

SUBJECT	The boy **who wins the race** will get the prize.
SUBJECT	The fine must be paid by **whoever holds the deed.**
SUBJECT	**Who** has the reader's sympathy, Huck or Jim?
OBJECT	Give this task to **whomever you trust.**
OBJECT	**Whom** can Cordelia trust as the scene ends?

21e Recognizing adjectives and adverbs

Adjectives and adverbs **modify** other words, adding to, qualifying, limiting, or extending their meaning.

FEATURES OF ADJECTIVES AND ADVERBS

ADJECTIVES

- Modify nouns and pronouns
- Answer "How many?" "What kind?" "Which one (or ones)?" "What size, color, or shape?"
- Include words like *blue, complicated,* and *good*
- Include words created by adding endings like *-able, -ical, -less, -ful,* and *-ous* to nouns or verbs (*sociological, nervous, seamless*)

ADVERBS

- Modify verbs, adjectives, and other adverbs
- Modify phrases (*almost* over the hill), clauses (*soon after* I added the eggs), and sentences (*Remarkably,* the mechanism was unharmed)
- Answer "When?" "Where?" "How?" "How often?" "Which direction?" "What degree?"
- Include mostly words ending in *-ly* (*quickly*) but also some words that do not end in *-ly* (*fast, very, well, quite, late*)

21f Editing adjectives and adverbs

Because not all adverbs end in *-ly* and some adjectives do (*friendly*), the *-ly* ending won't always help you pick the right form. If you can't tell which to use, ask the questions in the chart above.

DRAFT   Write **careful** so the directions are clear.

                    QUESTION: Write *how*? It answers an adverb question.

EDITED   Write **carefully** so the directions are clear.

STRATEGY   **Draw an arrow.**

Point to the word that is modified. If it acts as a noun or pronoun, select an adjective; if it acts as a verb, adjective, or adverb, use an adverb.

DRAFT   The insulation underwent **remarkable** quick deterioration

CONNECTION: *Remarkable* modifies *quick* (and answers the adverb question "How quick?"). (*Quick* in turn modifies *deterioration* and answers the adjective question "What kind of deterioration?") Replace *remarkable* with an adverb.

EDITED   The insulation underwent **remarkably** quick deterioration.

TRICKY ADJECTIVES AND ADVERBS

BAD/BADLY

Use *bad* (adjective) with linking verbs (*is, seems, appears*).
Use *badly* (adverb) with action verbs.

I feel **bad** that our group argues so much.
The new breathing apparatus works **badly.**

GOOD/WELL

Use *good* (adjective) with linking verbs (*is, seems*)
Use *well* (adverb) with action verbs unless it refers to health.

The chef's new garlic dressing tastes **good.**
The new pump works **well.**
Nan looks **well.** [health]

REAL/REALLY

Use *really* (adverb), not *real,* to modify an adjective or adverb.

Lu Ming is **really** efficient.
Lu Ming works **really** efficiently.

SURE/SURELY

Use *surely* (adverb) to modify an adjective.

This map is **surely** misleading.

Modifiers with linking verbs. Verbs such as *look, feel,* and *prove* can show both states of being (**linking verbs**) and activities (**action verbs**). Use an adjective for a state of being and an adverb for an activity.

ADJECTIVE (BEING)	The metal cover over the motor <u>turned</u> **hot**.
ADVERB (ACTION)	The large wheel <u>turned</u> **quickly**.
ADJECTIVE	The movement <u>grew</u> **rapid**. [The motion became quick.]
ADVERB	The movement <u>grew</u> **rapidly**. [The group spread its ideas.]

Real/really, bad/badly, good/well, sure/surely. Informal uses of these words may be accepted in speech but not in formal writing.

INFORMAL	I feel **badly** that our group argues so much.
	READER'S REACTION: Someone who *feels badly* has a poor sense of touch.

SERIOUS ERROR **Double negatives.** Readers are likely to feel that two negatives (*no, none, not, never, hardly, scarcely, don't*) cancel each other out.

DRAFT	The nurses **can't hardly** manage the emergencies.
	READER'S REACTION: This sounds more like a conversation than a report.
EDITED	The nurses **can hardly** manage the emergencies.

ESL ADVICE: Articles and Nouns

The **indefinite articles** are *a* or *an*; the **definite article** is *the*.

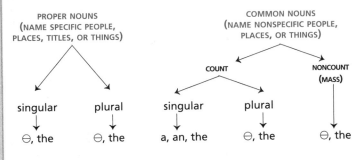

Singular proper nouns generally use no article, and **plural proper nouns** usually use *the*.

SINGULAR   Rosa Parks helped initiate the civil rights movement.

PLURAL   **The** Everglades have abundant wildlife.

Count nouns name individual items that can be counted: *two chairs, four cups, a hundred beans.*

Singular count nouns cannot stand alone. Use *a* or *an* when you are not referring to any specific person or thing. Use *a* before a consonant sound and *an* before a vowel sound.

I need **a** car to go to work. [unknown, nonspecific, or any car]

Use *the* when you are referring to an exact, known person or thing.

I need **the** car to go to work. [specific, known car]

Plural count nouns use either no article (to show a generalization) or *the* (to refer to something specific).

GENERALIZATION   Books are the best teachers.

SPECIFIC   **The** books on his desk are due Monday.

Noncount nouns (mass nouns) name material or abstractions that cannot be counted: *flour, water, steel.* Noncount (mass) nouns never use *a* or *an*. They may stand alone (when general) or use *the* (when specific).

GENERAL   Laughter is good medicine.

SPECIFIC   **The** laughter of children is good medicine.

Use *the* when a plural count noun or a noncount noun is followed by a modifier, such as an adjective clause or prepositional phrase, that makes the noun specific.

COUNT   **The** airline tickets that you bought are at half price.

NONCOUNT   **The** information on the flight board has changed.

21g Recognizing and editing comparisons

For most modifiers, choose the form based on how many things you compare: **positive** (no others), **comparative** (two things; *-er* or *more*), **superlative** (three or more things; *-est* or *most*). (See also p. 231.)

POSITIVE	The liquid flowed **quickly** into the **large** beaker.
COMPARATIVE	The liquid flowed **more quickly** into the **larger** beaker.
SUPERLATIVE	The liquid flowed **most quickly** into the **largest** beaker.

STRATEGY   Use precise comparative forms.

INACCURATE   Of the four age groups (20–29, 30–44, 45–59, and 60+),
those in the older group smoked least.

> **READER'S REACTION: Did those in the older *groups* or the
> *oldest group* smoke least?**

PRECISE   Of the four age groups (20–29, 30–44, 45–59, and 60+),
those in the **oldest group** smoked least.

Most readers won't accept double comparative forms.

DRAFT	Jorge is the **most agilest** athlete.
EDITED	Jorge is the **most agile** athlete.

Illogical comparisons. Some adjectives and adverbs, such as *unique, im-
possible, pregnant,* and *dead,* can't logically take comparative forms.

ILLOGICAL   Gottlieb's "Nightscape" is **most unique.**

> **READER'S REACTION: How can this painting be *more* or *most* if
> it's *unique*—the only one?**

LOGICAL   Gottlieb's "Nightscape" is **unique.**

PART 5 Writing Clearly

Voices
from the Community

"The difference between the almost right word and the right word is really a large matter—it's the difference between the lightning bug and the lightning." —Mark Twain, from a letter to George Bainton

22 | Clear Sentences

Most readers find murky or tangled sentences hard to read.

INDIRECT OR EVASIVE   It is suggested that employee work cooperation encouragement be used for product quality improvement.

READER'S REACTION: Who is suggesting this? What is "employee work cooperation encouragement"?

CLEAR   We will try to improve our products by encouraging employees to work cooperatively.

All communities value clear writing that's easy to read even if it presents complex ideas and reasoning. You can improve foggy sentences by creating clear subjects and verbs and using direct sentence structures.

22a Recognizing unclear sentences

Clear sentences answer the question "Who does what (to whom)?" When a sentence doesn't readily answer this question, try to make its subject and verb easy for readers to identify.

UNCLEAR   One suggestion offered by physicians is that there is a need to be especially observant of a baby's behavior in order to notice any evidence of seizures.

READER'S REACTION: Who's doing the observing?

CLEAR   Physicians suggest that parents watch babies carefully for evidence of seizures.

22b Editing for clear sentences

Readers need to identify subjects (who) and verbs (did what) easily.

STRATEGY **Find your significant subject.**

- Ask "Who (or what) am I talking about here?"
- Ask "Is this what I want to emphasize?"

UNFOCUSED   You run the greatest risk if you expose yourself to tanning machines as well as the sun because both can damage the skin.

READER'S REACTION: **Isn't the point the danger posed by sunbathing and tanning? Why are they both buried in the middle?**

EDITED   Either **the sun or a tanning machine** can damage the skin, and you run the greatest risk from exposure to **both** of them.

Weak nouns. When you create a noun (*completion, happiness*) from another kind of word such as a verb (*complete*) or an adjective (*happy*), you **nominalize** that word. Replace each weak nominalization with a clear and significant subject (or object). Name the action (did what?) in the verb. Avoid weak, lifeless verbs, especially forms of *be*.

In a **noun string,** one noun modifies another or nouns plus adjectives modify other nouns: *jet lag, computer network server.* Turn the key word in a string (usually the last noun) into a verb or a single noun. Then turn other nouns from the string into prepositional phrases.

CONFUSING   The team did a ceramic valve lining design flaw analysis.

EDITED   The team **analyzed** flaws **in** the lining design **for** ceramic valves.

Weak verbs. Forms of the verb *be* (*is, are, was, were*) show being, not action, and may create dull sentences.

STRATEGY **Energize your verbs.**

- Use more forceful verbs in place of forms of *be*.

WEAK   The program **is a money saver.**

STRONGER   The program **saves money.**

- Turn nouns into verbs to replace general verbs (*do, give, have, get, provide, shape, make*).

    WEAK   We **have done** a study of the project and **will provide** funding for it.

    STRONGER We **have studied** the project and **will fund** it.

- Drop indirect "there is," "there are," and "it is" patterns.

    DRAFT   **There is** a need for more classrooms at Kenny School.

    EDITED   Kenny School needs more classrooms.

ESL ADVICE: *There* and *It* as Subjects

There and *it* as subjects may not refer to a thing or place (as in *The car is there* or *What did it* [the book, for example] *say?*). *There* may introduce new material, and *it* may refer to weather, time, or distance.

DRAFT   Although there was snowing, it was dancing after dinner.

EDITED Although **it** was snowing, **there** was dancing after dinner.

Unnecessary passive voice. When you turn the doer or actor of a sentence into the receiver of action, you use the **passive voice** instead of the **active.** The passive voice focuses on the action, not the agent; the active voice puts the doer into the first, or subject, position.

STRATEGY Reconsider wordy or evasive passive structures.

PASSIVE **The people** affected by the toxin were contacted by **the Centers for Disease Control.**

ACTIVE   **The Centers for Disease Control** contacted the people affected by the toxin.

Separated subject and verb. Too much distance between a subject and verb can make a sentence difficult to read.

STRATEGY	**Keep the verb close to the subject.**
CONFUSING	The <u>veterinary association</u>, **in response to the costly guidelines for disposal of medical waste,** <u>has created</u> a low-cost loan program for its members.
EDITED	The <u>veterinary association</u> <u>has created</u> a low-cost loan program for its members **in response to the costly guidelines for disposal of medical waste.**

23 | Mixed Structures

When you're reading, you can't ask the writer to explain a confusing shift of topic or a jumbled sentence.

TOPIC SHIFT	One **skill** I envy is **a person** who can meet deadlines.
	READER'S REACTION: Does this mean a *skill* is a *person*?
EDITED	One **skill** I envy is **the ability** to meet deadlines.

Mixed sentences shift topics or grammatical structures unexpectedly, throwing the reader off the track. **Incomplete sentences** lack either grammatical (see 17a) or logical completeness. For example, if an advertiser says that *X* "is better," you expect to hear "than *Y*."

23a Recognizing mixed and incomplete sentences

In most sentences, the subject announces a topic, and the **predicate** (the verb and the words that complete it) comments on or renames the topic. With a **topic shift (faulty predication)**, the second part of the sentence comments on or names a topic different from the one first announced.

With a **mixed grammatical pattern,** the sentence shifts from one pattern to another.

> **STRATEGY**   Look for topic and comment.
>
> - Read your sentences aloud for *meaning*, especially how the topic (subject) and comment (predicate) relate.
> - Ask "Who does what?" or "What is it?" If the answer is illogical, edit.
> - Ask, "What's the topic? How does the rest of the sentence comment on it or rename it?"
> - Ask, "Does the sentence clearly tell who does what to whom?"
>
> TOPIC SHIFT   In this factory, **flaws** in the product noticed by any worker **can stop** the assembly line.
>
> READER'S REACTION: Who does what? Flaws can't stop the line.
>
> EDITED   In this factory, **any worker** who notices flaws in the product **can stop** the assembly line.

23b Editing mixed and incomplete sentences

State your topic; then imagine what readers will expect next.

> **STRATEGY**   Rename the subject.
>
> - Keep the topics on each side of *be* equivalent; make sure the second part of the sentence renames the topic in the first part.
>
> TOPIC SHIFT   **Irradiation** is **food** that is preserved by radiation.
>
> EDITED   **Irradiation** is a **process** used to preserve food.
>
> - Drop *is when* and *is where*; they create an imbalance on both sides of *be*.
>
> NOT BALANCED   **Blocking** is **when** a network schedules a less popular program between two popular ones.
>
> EDITED   **Blocking** is the **practice** of scheduling a less popular program between two popular ones.

• Rewrite to eliminate *the reason . . . is because.*

Readers expect the subject (topic) to be renamed after *is.* When *because* appears there instead, they find the sentence illogical.

DRAFT	The **reason** he took up skating **is because** he wanted winter exercise.
EDITED	The reason he took up skating **is that** he wanted winter exercise. [Change *because* to *that.*]
EDITED	He took up skating **because** he wanted winter exercise. [Drop *the reason . . . is.*]

Inconsistent sentence patterns. If you mistake words between the subject and verb for the sentence topic, you may mix up different patterns.

STRATEGY	Make the topic for subject and verb the same.
TOPIC SHIFT	Programming **decisions** by TV executives <u>consider</u> the need for audience share.
	READER'S REACTION: How can decisions think?
EDITED	When **making** programming decisions, **TV executives** <u>consider</u> the need for audience share.

Incomplete and illogical comparisons. You can sometimes simplify by omitting repeated elements that readers can supply. But if you cut essentials, you may create an **incomplete comparison**, missing words needed for clarity, or an **illogical comparison**, comparing things that aren't comparable.

STRATEGY	Add missing words or a possessive to compare logically.
ILLOGICAL	The fat content in even a small hamburger is more than a skinless chicken breast.
	READER'S REACTION: The fat is more than the chicken breast?
EDITED	The fat content in even a small hamburger is more than **that in** a skinless chicken breast.
EDITED	Even a small **hamburger's** fat content is more than a skinless chicken **breast's.**

24 | Dangling and Misplaced Modifiers

Readers generally expect to find related parts of a sentence together.

MISPLACED MODIFIER	The wife believes she sees a living figure behind the wallpaper in the story by Charlotte Perkins Gilman, which adds to her sense of entrapment. **READER'S REACTION: How could a story add to a feeling of entrapment?**
MODIFIER MOVED	The wife **in the story by Charlotte Perkins Gilman** believes she sees a living figure behind the wallpaper, which adds to her sense of entrapment.

Because a **modifier** qualifies, adds to, or limits the meaning of another word or word group, it needs to be positioned logically. Otherwise, readers may find a sentence vague, illogical, or even humorous.

 24a Recognizing misplaced modifiers

To recognize a **misplaced modifier,** look for a word or word group that is not positioned closely enough to the word or words it modifies—its **headword**—and instead appears to modify some other word.

MISPLACED	The caterer served food to the clients standing around the room on flimsy paper plates. **READER'S REACTION: Surely the clients weren't standing on the plates!**
MOVED	The caterer served food **on flimsy paper plates** to the clients standing around the room.

Dangling modifier. To spot a **dangling modifier,** look for a sentence that begins with a modifier but doesn't name the person, idea, or thing modified. Readers will think the modifier refers to the subject of the sentence that follows. If it doesn't, the modifier dangles.

DANGLING   **Looking** for a way to reduce complaints from nonsmokers, **a ventilation fan** was installed.

                   READER'S REACTION: How could a fan look for anything?

SUBJECT ADDED   **Looking** for a way to reduce complaints from nonsmokers, **the company** installed a ventilation fan.

Squinting modifier. To recognize a **squinting modifier,** look for a word that appears to modify both the word before and the word after. Squinting modifiers are often misplaced **limiting modifiers,** words like *only, almost, hardly, just, scarcely,* and *even.* Limiting modifiers can move around in a sentence, generally changing meaning as they do.

SQUINTING   People who abuse alcohol **often** have other problems.

                   READER'S REACTION: Do they *drink often* or *often have* other problems?

EDITED   People who **often** abuse alcohol tend to have other problems.

Split infinitives. Some readers find words placed between the parts of an infinitive (*to* plus a verb) irritating. Balance this risk against the directness a split infinitive sometimes offers.

IRRITATING?   The dancers moved **to very rapidly align** themselves.

EDITED   The dancers moved **very rapidly to align** themselves.

SERIOUS ERROR

24b Editing misplaced modifiers

Make sure modifiers clearly relate to the words they qualify.

STRATEGY Position and connect modifiers logically.

- Place *who, which,* or *that* close to its headword.

    MISPLACED The inspectors discovered another tank behind the building that was leaking toxic waste.

    MOVED **Behind the building,** the inspectors discovered another tank that was leaking toxic waste.

- State the word being modified.

    DANGLING While shopping, a stuffed alligator caught my eye.

    SUBJECT ADDED While **I was** shopping, a stuffed alligator caught my eye.

- Ask, "What do I really mean here? Who's doing what?" Then rework the sentence to state that point as directly as possible.

    DANGLING After debating changes in the regulations for months, the present standards were allowed to continue.

    READER'S REACTION: *Who* is debating? Not the standards!

    REWRITTEN The commission debated changes in the regulations for months but decided to continue the present standards.

25 | Unnecessary Shifts

Especially in formal contexts, readers expect logically consistent writing.

SHIFTED If **parents** called the school board, **we** could explain why **we** oppose the new policy.

READER'S REACTION: I'm confused. Who should do what?

EDITED If **parents** called the school board, **they** could explain why **they** oppose the new policy.

Although listeners tolerate shifts during conversation—or ask for clarification—readers are likely to be irritated by illogical shifts.

25a Recognizing shifts in person and number

A shift in **person** occurs when you switch illogically from one perspective (*I, you, he,* or *she*) to another. A shift in **number** occurs when you illogically switch sentence elements, especially pronouns and **antecedents** (the words to which they refer), between singular and plural.

INCONSISTENT   When **a business executive** is looking for a new job, **they** often consult a placement service.
READER'S REACTION: Who is "they"? The executive?

EDITED   When **business executives are** looking for **new jobs, they** often consult a placement service.

FIRST, SECOND, AND THIRD PERSON IN THREE COMMUNITIES

- **First person singular (*I*).** Use *I* to refer to yourself as the writer or person whose experiences and perceptions are an essay's subject. Readers may find *I* too personal in some formal academic contexts, especially in the sciences.
- **First person plural (*we*).** Use *we* in a collaborative project with several authors. In some academic papers, you may use *we* as you refer to ideas you and your readers share. *We* is common at work and in public when you represent or appeal to your organization.
- **Second person (*you*).** Use *you* to refer directly to the reader ("you, the reader"). In most academic and work writing, readers find *you* inappropriate, but some situations call for *you*, as in a set of instructions or a plain-language contract. In public writing that urges action, *you* can engage the reader in a civic appeal.
- **Third person (*he, she, it, they, one, someone,* and comparable pronouns).** Use these pronouns to refer to the ideas, things, and people you write about, including *people, person,* and names of groups (such as *students*). Avoid sexist use of *he* and *she*. Be alert to exclusionary uses of pronouns, such as inappropriately pitting *we* against *they*.

SERIOUS ERROR **25b** Editing shifts in person and number

Reflect a consistent perspective in person and number.

| **STRATEGY** | Match references, and edit for consistency. |

- Do nouns and pronouns refer to the same person?
- Are they consistently singular or plural?

| SINGULAR | If **a person** has some money to invest, **he or she** should seek financial advice. |
| PLURAL | If **people** have some money to invest, **they** should seek financial advice. |

25c Recognizing shifts in tense

The **tense** of a verb indicates time as past, present, or future (see p. 226). When you change tense within a passage, you signal a change in time and the relationship of events. Illogical shifts can mislead your readers.

| ILLOGICAL SHIFT | Scientists **discovered** nests that **indicated** how some dinosaurs **take care** of their young. |
| LOGICAL | Scientists **discovered** nests that **indicate** how some dinosaurs **took care** of their young. |

ESL ADVICE: Verb Tense and Expressions of Time

Use both verb tense and time expressions (*today, soon*) to show changes in time. Keep these consistent.

| INCONSISTENT | I **study** English last year, and now I **worked** for an American company. |
| EDITED | I **studied** English last year, and now I **work** for an American company. |

25d Editing shifts in tense

Shift tense because your account or convention requires the change.

| STRATEGY | Match your verbs to your intended time. |

**INCONSISTENT
SHIFT TO PRESENT**   We **had been searching** for a festival site when suddenly Tonia **yells,** "This is it!"

EDITED   We **had been searching** for a festival site when suddenly Tonia **yelled,** "This is it!"

Follow convention, and use present tense when you summarize or analyze events or information from a work such as a novel or film.

INCONSISTENT   As the novel begins, Ishmael **comes** to New Bedford to ship out on a whaler, which he soon **did.**

CONVENTIONAL   As the novel begins, Ishmael **comes** to New Bedford to ship out on a whaler, which he soon **does.**

26 | Parallelism

When you use consistent patterns, readers can follow your ideas easily and concentrate on your meaning because they know what to expect.

WEAK   Hal furnished his apartment with what he purchased at flea markets, buying items from want ads, and gifts from friends.
READER'S REACTION: This list seems wordy and jumbled.

PARALLEL   Hal furnished his apartment with **purchases from flea markets,
items from want ads,**
and **gifts from friends.**

Parallelism is the expression of similar or related ideas in similar grammatical form; it creates sentence rhythms and highlights ideas.

26a Recognizing faulty parallelism

Once you begin a parallel pattern, you need to complete it.

MIXED   Swimming is an exercise that **aids** cardiovascular fitness, **develops** overall muscle strength, and **probably without causing** injuries.

PARALLEL   Swimming is an exercise that **aids** cardiovascular fitness, **develops** overall muscle strength, and **causes** few injuries.

26b Editing for parallelism

When you place items in a series, pair, or list, make sure they have the same structure even if they differ in length and wording. With the seven coordinating conjunctions (*and, but, or, for, nor, so,* and *yet*), use parallelism to heighten similarities or contrasts.

MIXED   A well-trained scientist keeps a detailed lab notebook and the entries made accurately.

PARALLEL   A well-trained scientist keeps a **detailed and accurate** lab notebook.

Edit each series with the full sentence in mind. If the lead-in word can be the same, don't repeat it. If the lead-in words differ, include them.

INCOMPLETE The main character in the novel *Tarzan of the Apes* has appeared on television, films, and comic books.
               READER'S REACTION: I doubt he appeared *on* films and *on* comic books.

EDITED   The main character in the novel *Tarzan of the Apes* has appeared **on** television, **in** films, and **in** comic books.

STRATEGY Use parallelism to organize meaning.

•   Build up to a key point placed last in a series.

    To complete their campaigns, candidates need stamina, courage, and, most of all, **ambition.**

- List items in parallel form.

  These trends characterized the early 1960s:

    1. **A growing** civil rights movement
    2. **A developing** anticommunist foreign policy
    3. **An increasing** emphasis on youth in culture and politics

- Emphasize clusters of sentences and paragraphs.

  Each of us probably belongs to groups whose values conflict. **You may belong to** a religious organization that **endorses restraint in** alcohol use while **you also belong to** a social group that **accepts drinking. You may belong to** a sports team **that supports** competing and a club **that promotes** cooperation.

- Connect sections of an essay or a report.

  The opening for each paragraph can be a simple parallel element.

  One reason for approving this proposal now is . . .

  A second reason for acting is . . .

  The third, and most important, reason for taking steps is . . .

27 | Coordination and Subordination

Suppose you were editing a report with this passage.

California's farmers ship fresh lettuce, avocados, and other produce to supermarkets. They never send fresh olives.

READER'S REACTION: These sentences sound choppy. How do they connect?

Using **coordination,** you could give equal emphasis to the statements.

California's farmers ship fresh lettuce, avocados, and other produce to supermarkets**,** **but** they never send fresh olives.

Using **subordination,** you could show the relative weight of ideas.

California's farmers ship fresh lettuce, avocados, and other produce to supermarkets, **though** they never send fresh olives.

27a Recognizing coordination

Use coordination to link words, phrases, or clauses to emphasize their equal weight, balance the structure, or express addition or opposition.

CREATING AND PUNCTUATING COORDINATION

* Use *and, but, or, for, nor, so,* or *yet* (coordinating conjunctions). Precede them with a comma when joining two main clauses, word groups that could stand on their own as sentences (see p. 224).

  cut **and** hemmed   intrigued **yet** suspicious

  The new zoning board met**,** **but** it did not vote.

* Use pairs like *either/or, neither/nor,* and *not only/but also.*

  either music therapy **or** pet therapy

* Use a semicolon.

  Some customers fidgeted**;** others stared at the ceiling.

* Use conjunctive adverbs like *however, moreover, nonetheless, thus,* and *consequently* preceded by a semicolon.

  The managers could speed up the checkout lines**;** **however,** they seldom pay much attention to the problem.

* Use a colon.

  Magazine racks by the checkout counters serve a useful purpose**:** they give customers something to read while waiting.

EXPRESSING RELATIONSHIPS THROUGH COORDINATION

RELATIONSHIP	COORDINATING CONJUNCTION	CONJUNCTIVE ADVERB
addition	, and	; in addition, ; furthermore,
opposition or contrast	, but , yet	; in contrast, ; however, ; nonetheless,
result	, so	; therefore, ; consequently, ; thus,
cause	, for	
choice	, or	; otherwise
negation	, nor	

27b Recognizing subordination

Subordination creates sentences with unequal elements: the **main clause** (which could stand alone as a sentence) presents the central idea; at least one **subordinate clause** (which could not stand alone) modifies or comments on it. You signal this unequal relationship by beginning the subordinate clause with a **subordinator** or **relative pronoun,** a word like *while, although,* or *which,* and attaching it to the main clause.

CREATING AND PUNCTUATING SUBORDINATION

- **Use a subordinating conjunction** such as *although* or *because* to create a subordinate clause at the beginning or end of a sentence.

  At the beginning of a sentence: Add a comma *after* an introductory clause that begins with a subordinating conjunction.

  Once she understood the problem ⁹ she had no trouble solving it.

At the end of a sentence: Do not use a comma if the clause is *essential* to the meaning of the main clause (restrictive); use a comma if the clause is *not essential* (nonrestrictive). (See 30d.)

ESSENTIAL | Radar tracking of flights began **because several airliners collided in midair.**

NONESSENTIAL | The present air traffic control system works reasonably well**,** **although accidents still occur.**

- **Use a relative pronoun** (*who, which, that*) to create a relative clause at the end or in the middle of a sentence. A clause containing information *essential* to the meaning of the main clause begins with *that* and should not be set off with commas. Set off nonessential information. (See 30d.)

ESSENTIAL (NO COMMA) | The anthropologists discovered the site of a building **that early settlers used as a meetinghouse.**

NONESSENTIAL (COMMA) | At one end of the site they found remains of a smaller building**,** **which may have been a storage shed.**

EXPRESSING RELATIONSHIPS THROUGH SUBORDINATION

RELATIONSHIP	CONJUNCTION OR OTHER WORD
Time	before, while, until, since, once, whenever, whereupon, after, when
Cause	because, since
Result	in order that, so that, so, that
Concession or contrast	although, though, even though, as if, while
Place	where, wherever
Condition	if, whether, provided, unless, rather than
Comparison	as
Identification	that, which, who

27c Editing for coordination and subordination

How can you tell how much coordination or subordination to use? Read your writing aloud. Watch for short, choppy sentences or long, dense passages. Consider your community: academic readers may accept more subordination than work colleagues who favor conciseness.

STRATEGY	Replace *and, so,* and *but* to vary or specify.

DRAFT	The fresh grapefruit in supermarkets is picked before it matures to avoid spoilage, **and** it can taste bitter, **but** the grapefruit in cans is picked later, **and** it tastes sweeter.
EDITED	The fresh grapefruit in supermarkets is picked before it matures**,** **so** it can taste bitter. The grapefruit in cans is picked later **;** **consequently,** it tastes sweeter.

Help readers see what matters most; put key ideas in a main clause and secondary ideas in a subordinate clause.

STRATEGY	Move a main point to a main clause.

DRAFT	His equipment was inferior, although Jim still set a school record throwing the discus.
	READER'S REACTION: Isn't Jim's achievement the point?
EDITED	**Although** his equipment was inferior, Jim still set a school record throwing the discus.

ESL ADVICE Structures for Coordination and Subordination

Use both coordinators and subordinators, but don't mix the two.

MIXED	**Although** frogs can live both on land and in water, **but** they need to breathe oxygen.
CONSISTENT COORDINATION	Frogs can live on land and in water, **but** they need to breathe oxygen.
CONSISTENT SUBORDINATION	**Although** frogs can live on land and in water, they need to breathe oxygen.

28 | Conciseness

When you leave extra words in your writing, you waste the time of readers who value clarity, efficiency, or convincing advocacy.

WORDY   **There is evidence that the use of** pay **as an** incentive **can be a factor** in improvement **of the** quality **of** work.
            READER'S REACTION: Why is this so long-winded?

ABRUPT   Incentive pay improves work quality.

RESHAPED   Incentive pay **often encourages** work **of higher** quality.

Conciseness means using only the words you need—not the fewest possible, but only those that suit your purpose, meaning, and readers.

28a Recognizing common types of wordiness

Look carefully for both unnecessary and repetitive words.

Wordy phrases. Shrink wordy phrases to one or two words—or none.

COMMON WORDY PHRASES	
PHRASE	REPLACEMENT
due to the fact that	because
at the present moment	now
has the capability of	can
in a situation in which	when
as a matter of fact	[omit]
in my opinion	[omit]

All-purpose words. These sound serious, yet words like *factor, aspect, situation, type, field, kind,* and *nature* are often fillers, as are modifiers like *very, totally, major, great, really, definitely,* and *absolutely*.

WORDY	Young Goodman Brown is so **totally** overwhelmed by **his own** guilt that he becomes **extremely** suspicious of the people **all** around him. [22 words]
CUT	Young Goodman Brown is so overwhelmed by guilt that he becomes suspicious of the people around him. [17 words]
REWRITTEN	Young Goodman Brown's **overwhelming** guilt makes him **suspect everyone**. [9 words]

Redundant expressions. Redundant pairs (*each and every*) and phrases (*large in size*) say the same thing twice. Eliminate them.

WORDY	Because it was **sophisticated in nature** and **tolerant in style,** Kublai Khan's administration aided China's development in the 1200s.
CUT	Because it was **sophisticated and tolerant,** Kublai Khan's administration aided China's development in the 1200s.
REWRITTEN	Kublai Khan's **adept and tolerant administration** aided China's development in the 1200s.

28b Editing for conciseness

Edit expressions and patterns that lead to wordiness.

> **STRATEGY** Vary your cutting and trimming.
> - Cut or rewrite what you've already stated or clearly implied.
> - Reduce writer's commentary ("In my paper, I will show . . .").

- Compress or delete word groups beginning with *which, who, that*, and *of* by converting clauses to phrases, phrases to words.

> **CLAUSES**   Chavez Park, **which is an extensive facility in the center of town,** was named after Cesar Chavez, **who fought for migrant farmers' rights.**
>
> **PHRASES**   Chavez Park, **an extensive facility in the center of town,** was named after Cesar Chavez, **an advocate for migrant farmers.**
>
> **WORDS**   Chavez Park, **a downtown facility,** was named after **migrant advocate** Cesar Chavez.

- Highlight the key points in a passage that interprets or draws conclusions. Combine them as you drop remaining generalities; then add specific supporting detail.

> **WORDY**   **Glaciers** were of central importance in the **shaping of the North American landscape.** Among the many remnants of glacial activity are **deeply carved valleys** and **immense piles of sand and rock.**
>
> **COMBINED**   Glaciers carved deep valleys and left behind immense piles of sand and rock, shaping much of the North American landscape.
>
> **DETAILED**   Glaciers carved deep valleys and left behind immense piles of sand and rock, shaping much of the North American landscape in the process. **Cape Cod and Long Island are piles of gravel deposited by glaciers.**

29 | Language Choices

Every speaker of English uses a particular variety of the language—a **dialect**—shaped by region, culture, and home community.

HOME VARIETY   Miss Brill **know** that the lovers **making** fun of her, but she **act** like she **don't** care.

EDITED   Miss Brill **knows** that the lovers **are making** fun of her, but she **acts as if** she **doesn't** care.

In the communities where they're used, these varieties seem natural. In academic, work, and public settings, however, such variations are generally seen as "errors."

29a Recognizing and editing language varieties

A "rule" in one dialect may break a rule in another. In all language, the rules are structures and conventions that people in a group agree, unconsciously, to use. By **code-shifting,** you can substitute "standard edited American English" for your home language variety when you write a college essay, a letter to an official, or a company report.

> **STRATEGY** Look for "rules" in your home language.
>
> Rule in KY: Rule elsewhere:
> The lawn needs mowed.   The lawn needs <u>to be</u> mowed.

29b Recognizing and editing disrespectful language

Treat others fairly by eliminating sexist and discriminatory language. Avoid using *mankind* or *men* for humankind and words implying men in occupations (*firemen*). To replace *he, his,* or *him* for all people, try a plural construction (e.g., *their* rather than *his and hers* for *his*).

SEXIST   Every trainee brought **his** laptop with **him.**

AWKWARD   Every trainee brought **his or her** laptop with **him or her.**

BETTER   All trainees brought **their** laptops with **them.**

> **STRATEGY** Watch for stereotyped roles.
>
> **STEREOTYPED**   The OnCall Pager is **smaller than most doctors' wallets** and **easier to answer than phone calls from their wives.**
>
>   **READER'S REACTION: I'm a woman doctor, and I'm insulted. OnCall will never sell a pager in my office!**
>
> **EDITED**   The OnCall Pager **will appeal to doctors because it's small and easy to operate.**

Most readers won't tolerate unfair biases against groups of people.

DEMEANING   My paper focuses on the **weird** courtship rituals of a **barbaric** Aboriginal tribe in southwestern Australia.

     READER'S REACTION: Your paper sounds biased. How can you treat this topic fairly if you don't respect the tribe?

EDITED   My paper focuses on the unique courtship rituals of an Aboriginal tribe in southwestern Australia.

RACIST   The economic problems in border states are compounded by increasing numbers of **wetbacks** from Mexico.

     READER'S REACTION: This derogatory name is offensive. I object to characterizing a group of people this way.

EDITED   The economic problems in border states are compounded by increasing numbers of illegal immigrants from Mexico.

PART

6 Writing with Conventions

Voices
from the Community

"Parenthetical remarks (however relevant) are unnecessary."
—Frank L. Visco, *How to Write Good*

30 | Commas

Because a comma can join, separate, or disrupt, it's easy to misuse.

CONFUSING   During the study interviews were used to gather responses from participants, and to supplement written artifacts.

READER'S REACTION: I can't tell where ideas begin and end.

EDITED   During the study **,** interviews were used to gather responses from participants **,** and to supplement written artifacts.

Instead of sprinkling commas at pauses, consider your readers. Public and work communities that favor direct prose may expect the fewest commas, while academic readers are likely to expect formal comma usage.

30a Recognizing commas that join sentences

When you use *and, but, or, for, nor, so,* or *yet* (**coordinating conjunctions**) to link two word groups that can stand alone as sentences, place a comma *before* the conjunction. (Avoid a comma splice. See 18a.)

DRAFT   The rain soaked the soil and the mud buried the road.

EDITED   The rain soaked the soil **,** **and** the mud buried the road.

30b Editing commas that join sentences

Readers react more strongly if you omit a conjunction than a comma, but in formal texts they'll see both as errors. Even to join short main clauses, a comma is always acceptable but might be omitted informally.

STRATEGY Analyze the pair joined by a conjunction.

If you find main clauses that could stand alone before and after the conjunction, add a comma *before* the conjunction.

Apex tried to ship the order **,** **but** the truck was late.

If you find any other sentence element before or after the conjunction, do *not* separate that pair with a comma.

PAIR SPLIT	We sanded **,** and stained the old table.
EDITED	We **sanded** and **stained** the old table.
PAIR SPLIT	I used stain that was cheap **,** and easy to clean.
EDITED	I used stain that was **cheap** and **easy to clean.**

30c Recognizing commas that set off sentence elements

The simplest sentences need no comma.

noun phrase	verb phrase
The storm	developed quickly.

You may add a layer to the beginning with an **introductory expression** or interrupt a sentence with **parenthetical expressions** or **nonrestrictive modifiers** that add interesting detail. Set these off with commas.

INTRODUCTORY	**For nearly an hour ,** the rain drenched Old Town.
TRANSITION	**In addition ,** the hail caused damage.
INTERRUPTER	It broke **, I think ,** a dozen church windows.
CONJUNCTIVE ADVERB	We hope **, therefore ,** that someone starts a repair fund.

TAG QUESTION	We'll contribute**,** **won't we?**
CONTRAST	The windows' beauty touches all of us**,** **not just the church members.**
DIRECT ADDRESS	Recall**,** **friends of beauty,** that every gift helps.
NONRESTRICTIVE MODIFIER	The stained glass**,** **glowing like exotic jewels,** enriches us all.

30d Editing commas that set off sentence elements

Use two commas to enclose an expression in midsentence; use just one after an opening or before a closing expression.

Introductory elements. Readers expect a comma to signal where the introduction ends and the main sentence begins.

> **STRATEGY** | **Set off introductory wording for readability.**
>
> | | |
> |---|---|
> | **CONFUSING** | Forgetting to alert the media before the rally Jessica rushed to the park. |
> | **EDITED** | Forgetting to alert the media before the rally**,** Jessica rushed to the park. |

In general, put a comma after a long introductory element following a subordinating conjunction (*although*, *because*, *when*; see 27b), a preposition (*during*, *without*, *between*; see p. 232), or a verbal (see p. 229). Also add a comma if a short introductory element might confuse readers.

CONFUSING	By six boats began showing up.
EDITED	By six**,** boats began showing up.

Parenthetical expressions. Use commas to help readers identify word groups that interrupt a sentence.

DRAFT	Teams should meet even spontaneously as needed.
EDITED	Teams should meet**,** even spontaneously**,** as needed.

Nonessential, nonrestrictive modifiers. Midsentence modifiers act as adjectives or adverbs, adding detail that qualifies other words.

STRATEGY Test whether a modifier is essential.

Drop the modifier, and see whether the essential meaning of the sentence stays the same. If it does, even if it's less informative, the modifier is **nonrestrictive,** adding detail that's interesting or useful but not necessary for meaning. Set it off *with* commas so readers see it as nonessential.

DRAFT   Their band **which performs in small clubs** has gotten fine reviews.

TEST: Their band has gotten fine reviews. [The meaning is the same though it's less informative.]

COMMAS ADDED (NONRESTRICTIVE)   Their band **,** **which performs in small clubs ,** has gotten fine reviews.

If dropping a modifier eliminates essential information and changes the meaning of the sentence, the modifier is **restrictive.** Add it *without* commas so readers see it as a necessary part of the sentence.

DRAFT   The charts **,** **drawn by hand ,** were hard to read.

TEST: The charts were hard to read. [This says *all* the charts were hard to read but means that only *some* were.]

COMMAS OMITTED (RESTRICTIVE)   The charts **drawn by hand** were hard to read.

Who, which, and that. Add commas to set off nonrestrictive (nonessential) clauses beginning with *who, which, whom, whose, when,* or *where.* Because *that* can specify, rather than add, use it in restrictive (essential) clauses. *Which* often adds nonessentials but can be used either way.

NONRESTRICTIVE   Preventive dentistry **,** **which is receiving great emphasis ,** may reduce visits to the dentist's office.

RESTRICTIVE   Dentists **who encourage good oral hygiene** often supply helpful advice.

RESTRICTIVE   They also provide sample products **that encourage preventive habits.**

Appositives. An **appositive,** a noun or pronoun that renames a preceding noun, is usually nonrestrictive (nonessential). If so, add commas.

NONRESTRICTIVE   Amy Nguyen**,** **a poet from Vietnam,** published another collection of verse.

RESTRICTIVE   The well-known executive **Louis Gerstner** went from RJR Nabisco to IBM.

30e Editing disruptive commas

Unless you need to set off an intervening expression, you'll irritate readers if a comma separates subject and predicate.

STRATEGY Drop extra commas between subject and verb.

SPLIT SUBJECT AND PREDICATE   The painting *Rocks at L'Estaque***,** is in the Museu de Arte.

EDITED   The **painting** *Rocks at L'Estaque* **is** in the Museu de Arte.

Subordinating conjunctions (see 27b) shouldn't be followed by commas because they introduce entire clauses. Don't mistake them for conjunctive adverbs (such as *however;* see 27a) or transitional expressions (such as *for example*), which should be set off with commas.

STRATEGY Omit commas right after words like *because.*

EXTRA COMMA   Although**,** Jewel lost her luggage, she had her laptop.

EDITED   **Although** Jewel lost her luggage, she had her laptop.

30f Editing commas with words in a series

Use commas to separate or relate items in a series.

Series of three or more.   To avoid ambiguity, consistently use commas between all items of roughly equal status. If an item has multiple parts, place a comma after the entire unit.

> The Human Relations Office has forms for medical benefits **,** dental and vision options **,** **and** retirement contributions.

Although readers in the academic community frequently expect the comma just before *and*, it's often omitted, especially in a short, clear list.

Numbered or lettered list.   Punctuate a list in a sentence like a series; when items contain commas, separate them with semicolons (see 31c).

> You should (a) measure the water's salinity **,** (b) weigh any waste in the filter **,** and (c) determine the amount of dissolved oxygen.

Adjectives in sequence.   When you use **coordinate adjectives,** each modifies the noun (or pronoun) on its own. Separate them with commas to show their equal application to the noun. When you use **noncoordinate adjectives,** one modifies the other, and it, in turn, modifies the noun (or pronoun). Don't separate these adjectives with a comma.

STRATEGY   Ask questions about adjectives.

If you answer one of these questions with *yes*, the adjectives are coordinate. Separate them with a comma.

- Can you place *and* or *but* between the adjectives?

  COORDINATE (EQUAL)   Irrigation has turned dry **,** infertile [*dry and infertile?*— *yes*] land into orchards.

  NOT COORDINATE   The funds went to new computer [*new and computer?*— *no*] equipment.

- Is the sense the same if you reverse the adjectives?

  COORDINATE (EQUAL)   We left our small **,** cramped [*cramped small?*—*yes, the same*] office.

  NOT COORDINATE   We bought a red brick [*brick red?*—*no, could mean a color*] building.

COMMA CONVENTIONS

DATES

May 3, 1999   on Monday, June 23,   on July 4, 1776,
5 April 1973   October 2001   fall 2002   June 3

NUMBERS

1,746 sheep (or 1746 sheep) $8,543,234   page 2054

ADDRESSES AND PLACE NAMES IN SENTENCES

in Chicago   in Chicago, Illinois, during May
Fredelle Seed Brokers, Box 389, Holland, MI 30127

PEOPLE'S NAMES AND TITLES

Shamoon, Linda   Cris Burk, A.I.A., was the designer.

OPENINGS AND CLOSINGS OF LETTERS

PERSONAL   Dear Nan,   Dear Soccer Team,   Regards,
BUSINESS OR FORMAL   Dear Ms. Yun :   Sincerely,

---

31 | Semicolons and Colons

Semicolons and colons help readers make connections.

TWO SENTENCES   On April 12, 1861, one of Beauregard's batteries fired on Fort **Sumter. The** Civil War had begun.

> **READER'S REACTION:** These sentences may present facts or drama, but they don't *necessarily* connect events.

SEMICOLON	On April 12, 1861, one of Beauregard's batteries fired on Fort **Sumter ; the** Civil War had begun.

READER'S REACTION: The semicolon encourages me to link the battery firing to the Civil War beginning.

COLON	On April 12, 1861, one of Beauregard's batteries fired on Fort **Sumter : the** Civil War had begun.

READER'S REACTION: Now I see the guns' firing as a dramatic moment: the beginning of the Civil War.

You can use semicolons and colons to relate your ideas and to encourage readers to take different perspectives.

31a Recognizing semicolons that join sentences

A semicolon can dramatically highlight a close relationship or a contrast as it creates a brief pause.

TWO SENTENCES	Demand for paper is at an all-time high. Business alone consumes millions of tons each year.
ONE SENTENCE WITH SEMICOLON	Demand for paper is at an all-time high ; business alone consumes millions of tons each year.

31b Editing semicolons that join sentences

When you use a semicolon alone to link main clauses, you assume readers can figure out how the clauses relate. When you add words, you specify the connection for readers.

Assertion ; ⟶ transition , ⟶ assertion
I like apples ; **however** , I hate pears.

You can choose a **conjunctive adverb** (*thus, moreover*; see 27a) or a **transitional expression** (*for example, in contrast, on the other hand*). Vary the punctuation depending on where you place such wording.

BETWEEN CLAUSES	Joe survived the flood**;** **however,** Al was never found.
WITHIN CLAUSE	Joe survived the flood**;** Al**,** **however,** was never found.
AT END OF CLAUSE	Joe survived the flood**;** Al was never found**,** **however.**

STRATEGY Test both sides of the semicolon.

A semicolon joins main clauses that could stand on their own as sentences. Sometimes, elements in a second clause can be deleted if they "match" elements in the first clause even though the second couldn't stand alone.

ELEMENTS INCLUDED	In winter, the **hotel guests enjoy** a roaring log fire**;** in summer, the **hotel guests enjoy** the patio by the river.
ELEMENTS OMITTED	In winter, the **hotel guests enjoy** a roaring log fire**;** in summer, the patio by the river.

31c Editing semicolons in a complex series

When items in a series contain commas, readers may have trouble deciding which commas separate parts of the series and which belong within items. To avoid confusion, put semicolons between such items.

I met Debbie Rios, the attorney**;** Rhonda Marron, the accountant**;** and the new financial director.

31d Recognizing and editing colons

A colon effectively joins main clauses when the second clause focuses, sums up, or illustrates the first.

COLON WITH MAIN CLAUSES	The blizzard swept the prairie**:** the Oregon Trail was closed.

The words *before* the colon generally form a complete sentence while those after—the example, list, or quotation—may or may not.

COLON WITH LIST	The symptoms are as follows**:** cough, fever, and pain.

When you introduce a list with a word group other than a complete sentence, do not use a colon.

DRAFT   Her pastimes were **:** walking, volunteering, and cooking.

EDITED   Her pastimes **were walking,** volunteering, and cooking.

EDITED   **She had three pastimes:** walking, volunteering, and cooking.

Whether a quotation is integrated with your words or set off as a block (see 12b), a sentence must precede a colon. If not, use a comma.

COLON WITH QUOTATION   Dan answered his critics **:** "Sales are up and costs down."

COLON CONVENTIONS

Web Site Design **:** *A Beginner's Guide*   John 8 **:** 21–23

"Diabetes **:** Are You at Risk?"   http **:**//www.nytimes.com

10 **:** 32 a.m.   Dear Ms. Will **:** (business letter)   a ratio of 2 **:** 3

---

32 | Apostrophes

Like the dot above the *i*, the apostrophe may seem trivial, but without it, readers would stumble over your text.

MISUSED OR LEFT OUT   Though its an 1854 novel, Dickens *Hard Times* remain's an ageless critique of education by fact's.

READER'S REACTION: I can't tell possessives from contractions and plurals in this sentence.

EDITED   Though it's an 1854 novel, Dickens's *Hard Times* **remains** an ageless critique of education by **facts**.

In all three communities, readers see apostrophes as conventional, not flexible. Check carefully for them.

32a Recognizing apostrophes that mark possession

Nouns that express ownership are called **possessive nouns.** Mark them to distinguish them from plurals.

APOSTROPHE MISSING   The cats meow is becoming fainter.
> READER'S REACTION: I expected "The cats meow all night." Do you mean many cats or the meow of one cat?

APOSTROPHE ADDED   The **cat's** meow is becoming fainter.

> **STRATEGY**   Test nouns for possession.

If you can turn a noun into a phrase using *of*, use a possessive form. If not, use a plural.

DRAFT   The officers reports surprised the reporters.
> TEST: The reports *of* the officers? [*yes, possessive*]
> TEST: Surprised *of* the reporters? [*no, plural*]

EDITED   The officers' reports surprised the reporters.

32b Editing apostrophes that mark possession

Decide what to add: ' + -s or just '.

> **STRATEGY**   Check the ending of the noun.

- **Does the noun end in a letter other than -s? Add ' + s.**
  Ohio's taxes   the dog's collar   women's track

- **Does the noun end in -s, and is it plural? Add '.**
  the Solomons' car   buses' routes

- **Does the noun end in -s, and is it singular?**

  OPTION #1
  (PREFERRED)   Add ' + -s: Chris**'s** van

  OPTION #2   Add ' *after* the final -s: Chris**'** van

- **Does the noun end in -s and sound awkward?**

  OPTION #1   Hodges**'s** (sounds awkward as "Hodges-es")
                       Add ' but no -s: Hodges**'** (shows one -s sound)

  OPTION #2   Change the construction.

  DRAFT   the Adams County Schools**'s** policy

  EDITED   the policy of the Adams County Schools

Decide whether nouns joined by *and* or *or* act separately or together.

SEPARATE LAWYERS   **Bo's and Hal's** lawyers are ruthless.

SINGLE LEGAL TEAM   **Bo and Hal's** lawyers are ruthless.

Omit unnecessary apostrophes in other words that end in *s*.

VERB (NOT NOUN)   The staff **orders** supplies early.

PERSONAL PRONOUNS   If **your** car is here, why take **hers**?

APOSTROPHE CONVENTIONS

Dates   the **'**00s   the class of **'**05   1980s

Plural Letters and Numbers   p**'**s and q**'**s   size 10**'**s

Abbreviations   IQs   TAs

Dialect   I'm **a-goin'** for some **o'** them shrimp.

Hyphenated Noun   My **father-in-law's** library is huge.

Multiword Noun   The **union leaders'** talks collapsed.

32c Recognizing apostrophes that mark contractions

Informally, use an apostrophe to mark omitted letters when words are combined in a **contraction** (can't = can + not). In most academic writing, avoid splicing nouns with is (Zorr's testing = Zorr is testing).

32d Editing apostrophes that mark contractions

Some confusing contractions sound like other words.

they're = they + are   there = adverb

who's = who + is   whose = possessive pronoun

STRATEGY Expand contractions to test the form.

DRAFT **Its** the best animal shelter in **its** area.

EXPANSION TEST: *It is* [*yes, a fit*] the best animal shelter in *it is* [*no, not a fit*] area.

EDITED **It's** the best animal shelter in **its** area.

33 | Quotation Marks

Quotation marks set off someone else's spoken or written words.

DRAFT "Without the navigator," the pilot said, we would have crashed.

READER'S REACTION: Without quotation marks, I didn't realize that the pilot said the last part, too.

EDITED   66Without the navigator,99 the pilot said, 66we would have crashed.99

Readers in academic, work, and public communities expect you to position quotation marks to show who said what.

33a Recognizing marks that set off quotations

When you quote *directly*, use double quotation marks (" ") around the exact words quoted. (See 12b and 33b.) In dialogue, use new marks and indent when a new person speaks.

DIRECT QUOTATION
(SPOKEN)   66The loon can stay under water for several minutes,99 the ranger told us.

DIRECT QUOTATION
(WRITTEN)   Gross argues that 66every generation scorns its offspring's culture99 (9).

DIRECT QUOTATION
INTERRUPTED   66Every generation,99 so Gross claims, 66scorns its offspring's culture99 (9).

ESL ADVICE: Quotation Marks

Check for American conventions if your native language uses other marks for quotations or if you are used to British conventions. Search for these marks with your computer to spot unconventional usage.

33b Editing marks that set off quotations

When one quotation contains another, use single marks (' ') for the inside quotation and double marks (" ") for the one enclosing it.

QUOTATION
INSIDE
QUOTATION   De Morga's account described the battle that 66caused his ship to 6burst asunder9 99 (Goddio 37).

For quotation marks for emphasis, see 34b. For *indirect* quotations that paraphrase or sum up someone's words, omit quotation marks. (See 12d.)

PARAPHRASE (INDIRECT)   The pilot credited the navigator with the safe landing.

SUMMARY (INDIRECT)   Gross believes that, after just one generation, the social consequences of a major war nearly vanish (5).

COMBINING MARKS

- Position commas to help readers distinguish your introduction, commentary, or source from the quotation.

  "Our unity ‚ " said the mayor ‚ "is our strength."

- If your words end with *that*, don't include a comma.

  Some claimed that "calamity followed Jane." Jane replied that she simply outran it.

- Place these marks *inside* concluding single or double quotation marks: commas, periods, and question or exclamation marks that apply to the quoted material. Place these marks *outside*: semicolons, colons, and question or exclamation marks that apply to the whole sentence.

33c Editing quotation marks with titles of short works

Use quotation marks for titles of short works, parts of larger works, and unpublished works.

CONVENTIONS FOR TITLES

ITALICS OR UNDERLINING	QUOTATION MARKS
BOOK, NOVEL, COLLECTION	**CHAPTER, ESSAY, SELECTION**
The Labyrinth of Solitude	"The Day of the Dead"
The White Album	"Once More to the Lake"

ITALICS OR UNDERLINING	QUOTATION MARKS
PAMPHLET *Guide for Surgery Patients*	**SECTION** "Anesthesia"
LONG POEM *Paradise Lost* *The One Day*	**SHORT POEM, FIRST LINE TITLE** "Richard Cory" "Whoso list to hunt"
RADIO, TV PROGRAM *The West Wing* *Car Talk*	**EPISODE, REPORT** "Gone Quiet" "Daycare Dilemmas"
MUSICAL WORK, ALBUM *Messiah* *Invisible Touch*	**SECTION, SONG** "All We Like Sheep" "Big Money"

Organ Symphony BUT Symphony no. 3 in C Minor, op. 78

MAGAZINE, NEWSPAPER *Discover* the *Denver Post*	**ARTICLE** "What Can Baby Learn?" "Asbestos Found in Schools"
SCHOLARLY JOURNAL *Composition Review*	**ARTICLE** "Student Revision Practices"
PLAY, FILM, ART WORK *King Lear* *Winged Victory*	**UNPUBLISHED WORK, LECTURE** "Renaissance Women" "Sources of Heroic Ballads"

NO ITALICS, UNDERLINING, OR QUOTATION MARKS

SACRED BOOKS, PUBLIC OR LEGAL DOCUMENTS

Bible, Koran, Talmud, United States Constitution

TITLE OF YOUR OWN PAPER (UNLESS PUBLISHED)

The Theme of the Life Voyage in Crane's "Open Boat"

The Role of Verbal Abuse in The Color Purple

34 | Italics and Underlining

Type that slants to the right—italic type—emphasizes words and ideas. In handwritten or typed texts, <u>underlining</u> is its equivalent: <u>The Color Purple</u> = *The Color Purple*.

UNDERLINING   Alice Walker's novel <u>The Color Purple</u> has been praised and criticized since 1982.
READER'S REACTION: I can spot the title right away.

Some readers, including many college teachers, prefer underlining because it's easy to see. Observe your community's conventions.

34a Recognizing conventions for italics (underlining)

Italicize titles of most long, complete works (see 33c). Italicize names of specific ships, planes, trains, and spacecraft (*Voyager VI, Orient Express*) but not *types* of vehicles (Boeing 767) or *USS* and *SS* (USS *Corpus Christi*). Italicize uncommon foreign expressions (*omertà*) but not common ones (junta, taco). Italicize scientific names for plants (*Chrodus crispus*) and animals (*Gazella dorcas*) but not common names (seaweed, gazelle).

34b Editing for conventions that show emphasis

Use italics to focus on a term or a word, letter, or number as itself.

In Boston, *r* is pronounced *ah* so that *car* becomes *cah*.

Set off technical or unusual terms with quotation marks or italics.

In real estate, "FSBO" (pronounced "fizbo") refers to a home that is "for sale by owner."

You can—*sparingly*—use italics for emphasis or contrast or use quotation marks for irony, sarcasm, or distance from a term.

> **STRATEGY** **Rewrite to eliminate excessive emphasis.**
>
> In personal and informal writing, underlining may add "oral" emphasis.
>
> **INFORMAL** Hand the receipts to me.
>
> **MORE FORMAL** Give the receipts to me personally.

35 | Capitals

Readers expect capital letters to signal the start of sentences or to identify specific people, places, and things.

CAPITALS MISSING thanks, ahmed, for your file. i'll review it by tuesday.

> **READER'S REACTION: Email or not, missing capitals are distracting.**

CAPITALS IN PLACE Thanks, Ahmed, for your file. I'll review it by Tuesday.

Follow capitalization conventions to make reading easy.

35a Recognizing capitals that begin sentences

Capital letters begin both sentences and partial sentences (see 17c).

Pack for Yellowstone this July. Wildlife and wonders galore!

35b Editing capitals that begin sentences

When capitals are flexible, be consistent within a text.

STRATEGY **Adjust your capitals when you quote.**

Especially in the academic community, capitalize the first word in a quotation that is a complete sentence or that begins your sentence.

SENTENCE QUOTED	According to Galloway, "**T**he novel opens with an unusual chapter" (18).

Don't capitalize part of a quotation integrated into your sentence structure or interrupted by your own words.

INTEGRATED	Galloway notes that the book "**o**pens with an unusual chapter" (18).
INTERRUPTED	"**T**he novel," claims Galloway, "**o**pens with an unusual chapter" (18).

Sentence in parentheses. Capitalize the first word of a sentence that stands on its own, but not one placed *inside* another sentence.

FREESTANDING	By this time, the Union forces were split into nineteen sections. (**E**ven so, Grant was determined to unite them.)
ENCLOSED	Saskatchewan depends on farming (**t**he province produces over half of Canada's wheat), oil, and mining.

First word in a line of poetry. Traditionally, lines of poetry begin with capitals, but follow the poet's practice.

> **W**e said goodbye at the barrier,
>
> **A**nd she slipped away. . . .
>
> Robert Daseler, "At the Barrier," *Levering Avenue*

Questions in a series. Capitalize or lowercase the series.

OPTION #1	Do we need posters? **S**igns? **F**lyers?
OPTION #2	Do we need posters? **s**igns? **f**lyers?

Sentence after a colon. If a *sentence* follows a colon, choose capitals or lowercase. Otherwise, do not use a capital.

OPTION #1   The province is bilingual: **O**ne-third speak French and the rest English

OPTION #2   The province is bilingual: **o**ne-third speak French and the rest English.

Run-in list. When items in a list are not presented on separate lines, don't capitalize word groups or sentences.

NOT CAPITALIZED   Include costs for (a) **l**abs, (b) **p**hones, and (c) **s**upplies.

Vertical list. Capitalize sentences in vertical lists. Choose whether to capitalize word groups in an outline without periods.

OPTION #1   **OPTION #2**

1. **L**ab facilities   1. **l**ab facilities
2. **E**quipment   2. **e**quipment

35c Editing capitals that begin words

Capitalize names of specific people, places, and things (**proper nouns**) as well as related **proper adjectives**.

Brazil, Dickens   Brazilian music, Dickensian plot

In titles, capitalize first and last words, and all words between except articles (*a, an, the*), prepositions under five letters (*of, to*), and coordinating conjunctions (*and, but*). Capitalize the word after any colon.

The Mill on the Floss   "Civil Rights: What Now?"

Building a Small Business (your own title)

In an APA reference list, capitalize only proper nouns and the first letters of titles and subtitles of full works (see 14b).

CAPITALIZATION CONVENTIONS

CAPITALS	LOWERCASE
INDIVIDUALS, RELATIVES	
Georgia O'Keeffe, Mother	my cousin, her dad
PEOPLE, LANGUAGES	
Maori, African American	the language, the people
TIME PERIODS, SEASONS	
October, Ramadan	spring, winter, holiday
RELIGIONS, RELATED SUBJECTS	
Talmud, Bible, God	talmudic, biblical, a god
ORGANIZATIONS, INSTITUTIONS, MEMBERS	
U.S. Senate	a senator
Air Line Pilots Association	the union, a union member
PLACES, RESIDENTS, GEOGRAPHIC REGIONS	
Malaysia, the Southwest	the country, southwestern
BUILDINGS, MONUMENTS	
Taj Mahal, Getty Museum	the tower, a bridge
HISTORICAL PERIODS, EVENTS, MOVEMENTS	
Jazz Age, Postmodernism	the movement, a trend
ACADEMIC INSTITUTIONS, COURSES	
Harbor Community College	a university, the college
Sociology 203, Art 101	a philosophy course
COMPANY NAMES, TRADE NAMES, VEHICLES	
Siemens, Kleenex, Voyager	the company, tissues, van
SCIENTIFIC, TECHNICAL, MEDICAL TERMS	
Big Dipper, Earth (planet)	star, earth (ground)

36 | Abbreviations

When they are accepted by both writer and reader, abbreviations act as a kind of shorthand, making a sentence easy to write and read.

CONFUSING   **Jg. Rich.** Paret was a **U of C** law **prof.**

READER'S REACTION: What is "U of C"—the University of California?

CLEAR   **Judge Richard** Paret was a **University of Chicago** law **professor.**

Try to aid readers, not baffle them with inappropriate abbreviations.

36a Recognizing and editing abbreviations

Titles with proper names. Abbreviate a title just before or after a person's name. Use one form of a title at a time.

Jack Gill, **Sr.**   **Dr.** Vi McGee   Vi McGee, **D.D.S.**

ESL ADVICE: Abbreviated Titles

If titles such as *Dr.* or *Mrs.* do not require periods in your first language as they do in English, proofread carefully.

Spell out the title if it's part of your reference to the person or if it does not appear next to a proper name.

Professor Drew   Prof. Ann Drew   NOT Prof. Drew

Exceptions: Rev. Mills   Dr. Smith

Abbreviated academic titles such as *M.A.*, *Ph.D.*, *B.S.*, and *M.D.* can be used on their own or after a name.

People and organizations. Readers accept abbreviations that are familiar (IBM), simple (AFL-CIO), or standard in context (FAFSA). Most use capitals without periods.

Organizations	NAACP, AMA, GM, CNN, 3M
Countries	USA (*or* U.S.A.), UK (*or* U.K.)
People	JFK, LBJ, FDR, MLK
Things or Events	FM, TB, AWOL, DUI, TGIF

STRATEGY   **Introduce an unfamiliar abbreviation.**

Give the full expression when you first use it, and show the abbreviation in parentheses. Then, use just the abbreviation.

The **American Library Association (ALA)** studies policy on information access. The **ALA** also opposes censorship.

Dates and numbers. Abbreviations ($, no. for number) may be used with *specific* dates, numbers, or amounts.

AD	*anno Domini,* "in the year of Our Lord"
BC	*before Christ*
BCE	*before common era* (alternative for BC)
CE	*Common Era* (alternative for AD)
a.m. *or* A.M.	*ante meridiem,* "before noon" (A.M. in print)
p.m. *or* P.M.	*post meridiem,* "after noon" (P.M. in print)

36b Editing to use abbreviations sparingly

In research, scientific, technical, or specialized contexts, such as documenting sources, you can abbreviate more than in formal text.

CONVENTIONS FOR ABBREVIATIONS

- **In formal writing**

  Thursday, not Thurs.   Walton Avenue, not Ave

  Exception: 988 Red Road, Paramus, NJ 07652

  physical education   quart   mile   kilogram   chapter

  Exceptions: rpm, mph (with or without periods)

- **In tables or graphs:** @, #, =, −, +, other symbols

- **In documentation:** ch.   p.   pp.   fig.

- **In documentation and parentheses (from Latin)**

  e.g.: for example (*exempli gratia*)   i.e.: that is (*id est*)

  et al.: and others (*et alii*)   etc.: and so forth (*et cetera*)

---

37 | Numbers

You can convey numbers with numerals (37, 18.6), words (fifteen, two million), or a combination (7th, 2nd, 25 billion.)

GENERAL TEXT   These **fifty-two** chemists represent **thirty** labs.

> **READER'S REACTION:** In general academic texts, I expect most numbers to be spelled out.

TECHNICAL   These **52** chemists represent **30** labs.

> **READER'S REACTION:** In technical papers, I expect more figures.

Follow the advice here for numbers in general writing. In technical, business, and scientific contexts, seek advice from a teacher, supervisor, colleague, or style guide about conventional and consistent usage.

CONVENTIONS FOR NUMBERS IN GENERAL TEXT

- **Addresses and Routes**

  Interstate 6   2450 Ridge Road, Alhambra, CA 91801

- **Dates**

September 7, 1976	1880–1910	from 1955 to 1957
1960s	the sixties	the '60s (informal)
nineteenth century	AD (or CE) 980	class of '05

- **Times of Day**

10:52 6:17 a.m.	12 p.m. (noon)	12 a.m. (midnight)
four in the morning	four o'clock	half past eight

- **Parts of a Written Work**

  Chapter 12
  Genesis 1:1–6 or Gen.1.1–6 (MLA style)
  Macbeth 2.4.25–28 (or act II, scene iv, lines 25–28)

- **Measurements, Fractions, Decimals, Statistics**

120 MB	55 mph	6'4"	47 psi
21 ml	7-5/8	27.3	67 percent (or 67%)
7 out of 10	3 to 1	won 5 to 4	a mean of 23

- **Money**

  $7,883 $4.29 $7.2 million (or $7,200,000)

- **Rounded**

  75 million years   three hundred thousand voters

- **Ranges:** Simply supply the last two figures in the second number unless readers will need more to avoid confusion.

  34–45   95–102 (not 95–02)   370–420   1534–620

- **Ranges of Years:** Supply all digits for different centuries.

  1890–1920   1770–86   476–823   42–38 BC

- **Clusters:** items 2, 5, and 8 through 10 (or 8–10)

37a Recognizing when to spell or use numerals

In general, spell out numbers composed of one or two words, treating hyphenated compounds as a single word.

ten books   **twenty-seven** computers   **306** employees

37b Editing numbers in general text

Treat comparable numbers consistently in a passage, either as numerals (used for all if required for one) or as words.

CONSISTENT   Café Luna's menu soon expanded from **85** to **104** items.

STRATEGY   Spell out opening numbers, or rewrite.

INAPPROPRIATE   **428** houses are finished.

DISTRACTING   **Four hundred twenty-eight** houses are finished.

EASY TO READ   **In Talcott, 428** houses are finished.

38 | Hyphens

Readers expect hyphens both to join and divide words.

CONFUSING   The Japanese language proposal is well prepared.
                READER'S REACTION: Is the proposal *in* or *about* the Japanese language?

CLARIFIED   The Japanese-language proposal is well prepared.

Type a hyphen as a *single* line (-) with no space on either side: well-trained engineer, not well - trained engineer.

38a Recognizing hyphens that join words

A **compound word** is made from two or more words that may be hyphenated (*double-decker*), spelled as one word (*timekeeper*), or treated as separate words (*letter carrier*). Compounds change rapidly; check a current dictionary. Observe accepted practice in work or public contexts.

38b Editing hyphens that join words

Numbers. In general (not technical) writing, hyphenate numbers between twenty-one and ninety-nine (even if part of a larger one), inclusive numbers, and fractions: *fifty▬one thousand, volumes 9▬14, two▬thirds.*

Prefixes and suffixes. Hyphenate a prefix before a capital or number and with *ex-, self-, all-, -elect,* and *-odd: pre▬1989, self▬centered.*

Letters with words. Hyphenate a letter and a word forming a compound, except in music terms: *A▬frame, T▬shirt, A minor, G sharp.*

Confusing words. Use hyphens to help readers distinguish different words with the same spelling (*recreation, re▬creation*) or to clarify words with repeated letters (*anti▬imperialism, post▬traumatic*).

Compound modifiers. When two or more words work as a single modifier, generally hyphenate them *before* but not *after* a noun.

BEFORE NOUN (-)   Many **nausea▬inducing** drugs treat cancer.

AFTER NOUN (NO -)   Many drugs that treat cancer are **nausea inducing**.

Do not hyphenate *-ly* adverbs (highly regarded staff) or comparative forms (more popular products).

STRATEGY   Try suspended hyphens with modifiers.

Reduce repetition with hyphens that signal the suspension of an element until the end of a series of parallel compound modifiers. Leave a space after the hyphen and before *and*, but not before a comma.

     The lab uses **oil- and water-based** compounds.

38c Editing hyphens that divide words

Traditionally you could split a word at the end of a line, marking the break between syllables with a hyphen. Now word processors automatically hyphenate but often create hard-to-read lines or incorrectly split words. As a result, many writers turn off this feature. When you must divide an electronic address, do so after a slash. Don't add a hyphen.

39 | Spelling

Readers in all communities expect accurate spelling.

INCORRECT   The city will not **except** any late bids.

          READER'S REACTION: I get annoyed when careless or lazy writers won't correct their spelling!

PROOFREAD   The city will not **accept** any late bids.

Readers may laugh at a newspaper misspelling but harshly judge a writer who misspells in an academic paper or work document.

39a Using the computer to proofread for spelling

When you use a spelling checker, the computer compares each word in your text with the words in the dictionary in its memory. If it finds a match, it assumes your word is correct. If it does *not* find a match, it asks you if the word is misspelled. What it can't identify are words correctly spelled but used incorrectly such as *lead* for *led.*

39b Recognizing and editing spelling errors

Correct errors you see; ask readers to help you spot others.

STRATEGY Go beyond the spelling checker.

- Say the word carefully. Look up possible spellings, even odd ones. If you reach the right area in a dictionary, you may find the word.
- Try a dictionary for poor spellers that lists correct spellings (*phantom*) and likely misspellings (*fantom*).
- Try a thesaurus; the word may be listed as a synonym.
- Ask others for technical terms; verify their advice in a dictionary.
- Check the indexes of books on the word's topic.
- Look for the word in textbooks, company materials, or newspapers.
- Add a tricky word to your own spelling list. Invent a way to remember it (associating the two *z*'s in *quizzes* with boredom—*zzzzzz*).

Try to identify spelling patterns that will help you improve.

COMMON SPELLING PATTERNS

PATTERNS FOR PLURALS

WORD ENDING	CHANGE	EXAMPLES
most nouns	add -*s*	novel**s**, contract**s**
consonant + -*o*	often add -*es*	potato**es**, hero**es**
	some add -*s*	cello**s**, memo**s**
vowel + -*o*	add -*s*	stereo**s**, video**s**
consonant + -*y*	*y* to *i* + -*es*	gallery ⟶ galler**ies**
proper noun + -*y*	add -*s*	Kennedy ⟶ Kennedy**s**
vowel + -*y*	add -*s*	day**s**, journey**s**, pulley**s**
-*f* or -*fe*	often *f* to *v* + -*s*	life ⟶ li**ves**
	or -*es*	self ⟶ sel**ves**
	some add -*s*	belief**s**, roof**s**, turf**s**
-*ch*, -*s*, -*ss*, -*sh*, -*x*, or -*z* (a hiss sound)	most add -*es*	bench**es**, bus**es**, fox**es**, kiss**es**, buzz**es**
one-syllable ending in -*s* or -*z*	many double final consonant	quiz ⟶ qui**zz**es

WORD ENDING	CHANGE	EXAMPLES
foreign roots	follow original language	dat**um** ⟶ dat**a** criteri**on** ⟶ criteri**a**
irregular nouns		foot ⟶ f**ee**t
compound	last word	basketball**s**
	first word if most important	sister-in-law ⟶ sister**s**-in-law

PATTERNS FOR BEGINNINGS (PREFIXES)

Prefixes do not change the spelling of the root word that follows: *precut, post-traumatic, misspell, unendurable.*

PREFIX FOR *NOT*	COMBINATION	EXAMPLES
im-	with *b, m, p*	**im**patient, **im**balance
in-	with others	**in**correct, **in**adequate

PATTERNS FOR ENDINGS (SUFFIXES)

Suffixes may change the root word or pose other problems.

SUFFIX	CHANGE	EXAMPLES
starts with consonant	keep silent -*e*	fat**e**ful, gentl**e**ness
	exceptions	judgment, truly, argument, ninth
starts with vowel	drop silent -*e*	imaginary, generation, decreasing, definable
	exceptions	notic**e**able, chang**e**able

SUFFIX	COMBINATION	EXAMPLES
-ery	4 common words	station**ery** (paper), cemet**ery**, monast**ery**, millin**ery**
-ary	most others	station**ary** (fixed in place), secret**ary**, prim**ary**, milit**ary**
" seed" sound	most use -*cede*	pre**cede**, re**cede**
	several use -*ceed*	pro**ceed**, suc**ceed**, ex**ceed**
	one uses -*sede*	super**sede**

SUFFIX	COMBINATION	EXAMPLES
-able	add if root stands on own	charit**able,** advis**able**
with *-ee* root	keep *-e*	agree**able**
-ible	add if root can't stand on own	cred**ible,** irreduc**ible**

PATTERNS FOR SEQUENCES OF LETTERS WITHIN WORDS

LETTER GROUP	SEQUENCE	EXAMPLES
ie	*i* before *e* except after *c,* or sounding like *a* as in n**ei**ghbor and w**ei**gh.	bel**ie**ve, gr**ie**f, fr**ie**nd re**cei**ve, de**cei**t
	exceptions	an**cie**nt w**ei**rd, s**ei**ze, for**ei**gn, h**ei**ght, th**ei**r, **ei**ther, n**ei**ther, l**ei**sure

The Glossary also lists **homophones,** different words that sound alike.

COMMONLY CONFUSED WORD PAIRS

WORD	MEANING	WORD	MEANING
all ready	prepared	already	by this time
its	possessive of *it*	it's	*it is*
than	compared with	then	next
their	possessive of *they*	there	in that place
whose	possessive of *who*	who's	*who is*
your	possessive of *you*	you're	*you are*

40 | Other Marks and Conventions

You can use punctuation marks to change the style and sense of your prose and adjust its effects on readers.

DASHES   The boy—**clutching his allowance**—came to the store.

     READER'S REACTION: Dashes show strong emphasis; I can tell how hard the boy worked to save his money.

PARENTHESES   The boy (**clutching his allowance**) came to the store.

     READER'S REACTION: Parentheses deemphasize his savings, thus giving his arrival more significance.

COMMAS   The boy, **clutching his allowance,** came to the store.

     READER'S REACTION: This direct account doesn't emphasize either the savings or the arrival.

Punctuation marks set boundaries, guide readers, and add emphasis.

40a Recognizing and editing parentheses

Parentheses *enclose*: you can't use just one, and readers will interpret whatever falls between the pair as an aside.

 When you sign up for Telepick (including Internet access), you will receive an hour of free calls.

When parentheses *inside a sentence* come at the end, punctuate *after* the closing mark. When you enclose a *freestanding sentence*, punctuate *inside* the closing mark.

INSIDE SENTENCE   People on your list get discounts (once they sign up).

SEPARATE SENTENCE   Try Telepick now. (This offer excludes international calls.)

You can use parentheses to mark numbered or lettered lists.

NUMBERED LIST   Fax Harry's Bookstore (555-0934) to (1) order books, (2) inquire about items, or (3) sign up for events.

40b Recognizing and editing dashes

Too many may strike academic readers as informal, but dashes can add flair to work and public appeals, ads, or brochures. Type a dash as two un-spaced hyphens, without space before or after: --. A print dash appears as a single line: —. Use one dash with an idea or series that opens or ends a sentence; use a pair to enclose words in the middle.

OPENING LIST   **Extended visiting hours, better meals, and more exercise**—these were the inmates' demands.

PAIR IN THE MIDDLE   For her service to two groups—**Kids First and Food Basket**—Olivia was voted Volunteer of the Year.

STRATEGY Convert excessive dashes to other marks.

Circle dashes that seem truly valuable—maybe marking a key point. Replace others with commas, parentheses, colons, or emphatic wording.

40c Recognizing and editing brackets

Academic readers expect you to use brackets scrupulously (though other readers may find them pretentious). When you add your words to a quotation for clarity or background, bracket this **interpolation**. Also bracket *sic* (Latin for "thus") after a source error to confirm your accuracy.

INTERPOLATION   As Walz notes, "When Catholic Europe adopted the new Gregorian calendar in 1582, Protestant England still followed October 4 by October 5 [Julian calendar]" (4).

40d Recognizing and editing ellipses

The **ellipsis** uses three *spaced* periods to mark where something has been left out. Academic readers expect ellipses to mark omissions of irrelevant material from quotations; other readers may prefer full quotations.

CONVENTIONS FOR ELLIPSIS MARKS

- Use three spaced periods • • • for ellipses in a sentence or within a line of poetry.
- Use a period before an ellipsis ending a sentence• • • •
- Leave a space before the first period • • • and after the last unless the ellipsis is bracketed.
- Omit ellipses when you begin quotations (unless needed for clarity) or use clearly incomplete words or phrases.
- Retain another punctuation mark before omitted words if needed for the sentence structure; • • • omit it otherwise.
- Supply a series of spaced periods (MLA style) to show an omitted line (or more) of poetry in a block quotation.
- When quoting a text that uses ellipses, bracket your ellipses [• • •] in MLA style.

When you drop *part* of a sentence, maintain normal sentence structure so readers can follow the passage.

INTERVIEW NOTES   Museum Director: "We expect the Inca pottery in our special exhibit to attract historians from as far away as Chicago, while the vivid jewelry draws the public."

CONFUSING DRAFT   The museum director hopes "the Inca pottery • • • historians • • • vivid jewelry • • • public."

EDITED   The museum director "expect[s] the Inca pottery • • • to attract historians • • • while the vivid jewelry draws the public."

In narrative, ellipses can show a pause or ongoing action.

FOR SUSPENSE   Large paw prints led to the tent• • • •

40e Recognizing and editing slashes

You can use a slash to mark alternatives (the **on/off** switch), especially in technical documents, but readers may find it informal or imprecise (preferring *or* instead). When you quote poetry *within* your text, separate lines of verse with a slash, typing a space before and after.

> The speaker in Sidney's sonnet hails the moon: "O Moon, thou climb'st the skies! **/** How silently . . ." (lines 1–2).

40f Recognizing and editing end marks

Speakers change pitch or pause to mark sentence boundaries. Writers use symbols—period, question mark, exclamation point.

LESS FORMAL   And why do we need you? You help our lovable pups find new families!

READER'S REACTION: This bouncy style is great for the volunteer brochure but not the annual report.

MORE FORMAL   The League's volunteers remain our most valuable asset, matching abandoned animals with suitable homes.

Readers in all communities expect periods to end sentences. Some readers may accept informal use of question marks and exclamation points.

Periods. All sentences that are *statements* end with periods—even if they contain embedded clauses that report, rather than ask, questions. Periods also mark decimal points (5•75) and abbreviations (Dr•, Ms•, pp•, etc•, a•m•) though many abbreviations, pronounced as words or by letter, don't require them (NASA, GOP, OH).

Question marks. End a direct question with a question mark, but use a period to end an **indirect question**—a sentence with an embedded clause that asks a question.

DIRECT   When is the train leaving**?**

DIRECT: QUOTED   Lu asked, "Why is it so hot**?**"

DIRECT: TWO   Considering that the tax break has been widely publicized,
CLAUSES   why have so few people filed for a refund**?**

INDIRECT   Jose asked if we needed help**.**

Exclamation points. These marks end emphatic statements such as commands or warnings but are rarely used in academic or work writing.

EMPHATIC   Get the campers off the cliff**!**

> **STRATEGY**   Use draft punctuation to guide your editing.

Like question marks, exclamation points can be used informally, expressing dismay, shock, or strong interest. Edit for strong words to emphasize.

DRAFT   Rescuers spent hours (**!**) trying to reach the child.

EDITED   Rescuers spent **agonizing** hours trying to reach the child.

40g Recognizing and editing electronic addresses

When you cite an electronic address, record its characters exactly—including slashes, @ ("at") signs, underscores, colons, and periods.

  http**:**//www**.**access**.**gpo**.**gov**/**su__docs

40h Combining marks

* **Always use marks that enclose in pairs**.

    ( )   [ ]   " "   ' '

Use commas and dashes in pairs to enclose midsentence elements. Type a dash as a pair——of hyphens.

- **Use multiple marks when each mark plays its own role**. If an abbreviation with a period falls in the *middle* of a sentence, the period may be followed by another mark, such as a comma, dash, colon, or semicolon.

  Experts spoke until 10 **p•m•** , and we left at 11 **p•m•**

- **Eliminate multiple marks when their roles overlap**. When an abbreviation with a period concludes a sentence, that one period will also end the sentence. Omit a comma *before* midsentence parentheses; *after* the parentheses, use whatever mark would otherwise occur.

- **Avoid confusing duplicates**. If items listed in a sentence include commas, separate them with semicolons, not more commas.

  ___ **,** ___ **,** ___ **;** ___ **,** ___ **,** ___ **;** and ___ **•**

  If one parenthetical element falls within another, use brackets to enclose the unit inside the parentheses.

  _____ (___ [___] ___)**•**

Use one pair of dashes at a time, not dashes within dashes.

Grammar at a Glance

How can you recognize a sentence?

A **sentence**—also called a **main (or independent) clause**—is a word group that can stand alone. It has a subject and a predicate (a verb and any words that complete it).

SENTENCE   **Hungry bears** <u>were hunting</u> food.

SENTENCE   Because spring snows had damaged many plants, **hungry bears** <u>were hunting</u> food in urban areas.

A **subordinate (or dependent) clause** has a subject and a predicate, yet it cannot stand on its own because it begins with a subordinating word like *because, although, which,* or *that* (see 27b).

FRAGMENT   Because **spring snows** <u>had damaged</u> many plants

A **phrase** is a word group that lacks a subject, a predicate, or both. It cannot stand alone.

FRAGMENT   were hunting   in urban areas   the hungry bears

For further help in recognizing sentences, turn to Chapter 17 on fragments. See also Chapter 18 on comma splices and fused sentences.

HOW DO WORDS WORK IN SENTENCES?	
You can recognize	**By looking for words that do this**
nouns	name a person, a place, an idea, or a thing (*Jed, cafeteria, doubt, chair*)
pronouns	take the place of a noun (*them, she, his*)
verbs	express action (*jump, write*), occurrence (*become, happen*), and being (*be, seem*)
adverbs	modify or qualify verbs, adjectives, and other adverbs telling when, where, how, how often, which direction, or what degree (*now, very, quite, too, quickly*)
adjectives	modify or qualify nouns and pronouns, telling how many, what kind, which one, what size, what color, or what shape (*five, many, attractive, blue, young*)

prepositions	add information by linking the noun or pronoun following to the rest of the sentence (*after, at, in, by, on, near, with*)
conjunctions	join other words, signaling their relationships (*and, but, because, though*)
interjections	convey a strong reaction or emotion (*Oh, no! Hey!*)

How do sentence patterns work?

Five basic predicate structures

1. Subject + intransitive verb

The bus crashed.

2. Subject + transitive verb + direct object

A passenger called the police.

3. Subject + transitive verb + indirect object + direct object

The paramedic gave everyone a blanket.

4. Subject + transitive verb + direct object + object complement

Officials found the driver negligent.

5. Subject + linking verb + subject complement

The quick-thinking passenger was a hero.

Four sentence structures

1. A **simple sentence** has one main (independent) clause and no subordinate (dependent) clauses.

The mayor proposed an expansion of city hall.

2. A **compound sentence** has two or more main (independent) clauses and no subordinate (dependent) clauses (see 27a).

       main clause   main clause
Most people praised the plan, yet **some found it** dull.

3. A **complex sentence** has one main (independent) clause and one or more subordinate (dependent) clauses (see 27b).

      subordinate clause   main clause

Because people objected, **the architect revised the plans.**

4. A **compound-complex sentence** has two or more main (independent) clauses and one or more subordinate (dependent) clauses.

     subordinate clause   subordinate clause

Because he wanted to make sure that the expansion did not damage

                    main clause

the existing building, **the architect examined the older**

                    main clause

structure, and **he asked the contractor to test the soil stability.**

Four sentence purposes

A **declarative sentence** makes a statement: The motor is making a rattling noise. An **interrogative sentence** poses a question: Have you checked it for overheating? An **imperative sentence** requests or commands: Check it again. An **exclamatory sentence** exclaims: It's on fire!

What are the principal parts of verbs?

BASE FORM	PAST	PRESENT PARTICIPLE	PAST PARTICIPLE
REGULAR VERBS			
live	lived	living	lived
IRREGULAR VERBS			
eat	ate	eating	eaten
run	ran	running	run

What are the tenses of verbs in the active voice?

Decide when actions or events occur; then use this chart to help you select the tense you need for a regular (*examine*) or irregular (*begin*) verb.

Present, past, and future (showing simple actions)

Present: action taking place now, including habits and facts occurring all the time

I/you/we/they	examine/begin
he/she/it	examines/begins

Past: action that has already taken place at an earlier time

I/you/he/she/it/we/they	examined/began

Future: action that will take place at an upcoming time

I/you/he/she/it/we/they	will examine/begin

Present, past, and future perfect (showing order of events)

Present Perfect: action that has recurred or has continued from the past to the present

I/you/we/they	have examined/begun
he/she/it	has examined/begun

Past Perfect: action that had already taken place before something else happened

I/you/he/she/it/we/they	had examined/begun

Future Perfect: action that will have taken place by the time something else happens

I/you/he/she/it/we/they	will have examined/begun

Present, past, and future progressive (showing action in progress)

Present Progressive: action that is in progress now, at this moment

I	am examining/beginning
you/we/they	are examining/beginning
he/she/it	is examining/beginning

Past Progressive: action that was in progress at an earlier time

I/he/she/it	was examining/beginning
you/we/they	were examining/beginning

Future Progressive: action that will be in progress at an upcoming time

I/you/he/she/it/we/they   will be examining/beginning

Present, past, and future perfect progressive (showing the duration of action in progress)

Present Perfect Progressive: action that has been in progress up to now

I/you/we/they   have been examining/beginning
he/she/it   has been examining/beginning

Past Perfect Progressive: action that had already been in progress before something else happened

I/you/he/she/it/we/they   had been examining/beginning

Future Perfect Progressive: action that will have been in progress by the time something else happens

I/you/he/she/it/we/they   will have been examining/beginning

How can you recognize active and passive verbs?

Verbs in the **active voice** appear in sentences in which the doer (or agent) of an action is the subject of the sentence.

	DOER (SUBJECT)	ACTION (VERB)	GOAL (OBJECT)
ACTIVE	The car	**hit**	the lamppost.
ACTIVE	Dana	**distributed**	the flyers.

A verb in the **passive voice** adds a form of *be* as a helping verb to the past participle form. The subject (or doer) may appear as an object after the word *by* in an optional prepositional phrase. (See 22b.)

	GOAL (SUBJECT)	ACTION (VERB)	[DOER: PREPOSITIONAL PHRASE]
PASSIVE	The lamppost	**was hit**	[by the car].
PASSIVE	The flyers	**were distributed**	[by Dana].

What are verbal phrases?

Three verb parts—participles, gerunds, and infinitives—are known as **verbals**. They can function as nouns, adjectives, or adverbs, but they can never stand alone as verbs.

1. Build **participial phrases** with *-ing* (present participle) or *-ed/-en* (past participle) forms, using them as adjectives.

   Few neighbors **attending the meeting** owned dogs.
   They signed a petition **addressed to the mayor.**

2. Build a **gerund phrase** around the *-ing* form (present participle) used as a noun.

   Closing the landfill may keep it from **polluting the stream.**

3. Build an **infinitive phrase** around the *to* form, using it as an adjective, adverb, or noun.

   He used organic methods **to raise his garden.**
   To live in the mountains was his goal.

What are the forms of some common irregular verbs?

PRESENT	PAST	PAST PARTICIPLE
arise	arose	arisen
be	was/were	been
begin	began	begun
bite	bit	bitten/bit
bring	brought	brought
come	came	come
do	did	done
drink	drank	drunk
eat	ate	eaten
fly	flew	flown
go	went	gone
lay	laid	laid
lie	lay	lain
ride	rode	ridden

PRESENT	PAST	PAST PARTICIPLE
run	ran	run
see	saw	seen
set	set	set
sing	sang	sung
sit	sat	sat
take	took	taken
write	wrote	written

What do pronouns do?

- **Personal pronouns:** Designate persons or things using a form reflecting the pronoun's role in the sentence (see 21c).

SINGULAR	*I, me, you, he, him, she, her, it*
PLURAL	*we, us, you, they, them*

- **Possessive pronouns:** Show ownership (see 32a–b on apostrophes).

SINGULAR	*my, mine, your, yours, her, hers, his, its*
PLURAL	*our, ours, your, yours, their, theirs*

- **Relative pronouns:** Introduce subordinate clauses that act as adjectives and answer the questions "What kind of?" and "Which one?"

  who, whom, whose, which, that

- **Interrogative pronouns:** Introduce questions.

  who, which, what

- **Reflexive pronouns:** End in -self or -selves and enable the subject or doer also to be the receiver of an action.

- **Intensive pronouns:** End in -self or -selves and add emphasis.

SINGULAR	*myself, yourself, herself, himself, itself*
PLURAL	*ourselves, yourselves, themselves*

- **Demonstrative pronouns:** Point out or highlight an antecedent, refer to a noun or a pronoun, or sum up an entire phrase or clause.

  this, that, these, those

- **Reciprocal pronouns:** Refer to individual parts of a plural antecedent.
  one another, each other

- **Indefinite pronouns:** Refer to people, things, and ideas in general rather than to a specific antecedent (e.g., *anyone, both, each, few, none*).

What are the forms of comparatives and superlatives?

Adjectives

One syllable: Most add *-er* and *-est* (*pink, pinker, pinkest*).
Two syllables: Many add *-er* and *-est*; some add either *-er* and *-est* or *more* and *most* (*foggy, foggier, foggiest; more foggy, most foggy*).
Three (or more) syllables: Add *more* and *most* (*plentiful, more plentiful, most plentiful*).

Adverbs

One syllable: Most add *-er* and *-est* (*quick, quicker, quickest*).
Two (or more) syllables: Most add *more* and *most* (*carefully, more carefully, most carefully*).

Negative comparisons (adjectives and adverbs)

Use *less* and *least* (*less full, least full; less slowly, least slowly*).

Irregular forms

ADJECTIVE	COMPARATIVE	SUPERLATIVE
bad	worse	worst
good, well (healthy)	better	best
ill (harsh, unlucky)	worse	worst
a little	less	least
many, much, some	more	most
badly, ill (badly)	worse	worst
well (satisfactorily)	better	best

ESL ADVICE: How Do You Choose a Preposition?

Prepositions of time: *at*, *on*, and *in*

- Use *at* for a specific time. Use *on* for days and dates. Use *in* for nonspecific times during a day, month, season, or year.

  Brandon was born **at** 11:11 a.m. **on** a Monday **in** 1996.

Prepositions of place: *at*, *on*, and *in*

- Use *at* for specific addresses. Use *on* for names of streets, avenues, and boulevards. Use *in* for areas of land—states, countries, continents.

  She lives **on** Town Avenue but works **at** 99 Low Street **in** Dayton.

  Arrange prepositional phrases in this order: place, then time.

  The runners will start **in the park** on Saturday.

***To* or no preposition to express going to a place**

- When you express the idea of going to a place, use the preposition *to*.

  I am going **to** work.   I am going **to** the office.

- In some cases, use no preposition: I am going home.

***For* and *since* in time expressions**

- Use *for* with an amount of time (minutes, hours, days, months, years) and *since* with a specific date or time.

  The housing program has operated **for** many years, **since** 1971.

Prepositions with nouns, verbs, and adjectives

- Nouns, verbs, and adjectives may appear with certain prepositions.

  NOUN + PREPOSITION   He has an <u>understanding</u> **of** global politics.

  VERB + PREPOSITION   Managers <u>worry</u> **about** many things.

Glossary of Usage and Terms

This glossary includes matters of usage (words that writers often find confusing or difficult, such as *farther* and *further*), grammatical terms (such as *verb*), and rhetorical terms (such as *indirect quotation*).

a, an Use *an* before a vowel (*an old film*) or silent *h* (*an honor*) and *a* before a consonant (*a classic, a hero*) (See pp. 158–159.)

accept, except *Accept* means "to take or receive"; *except* means "excluding."

Everyone **accepted** the invitation **except** Larry.

active voice (See **voice.**)

adverse, averse Someone opposed to something is *averse* to it; *adverse* conditions oppose achieving a goal.

advice, advise *Advice*, a noun, means "counsel" or "recommendations." *Advise*, a verb, means "to counsel or recommend."

He tried to **advise** students who wanted no **advice.**

affect, effect The verb *affect* means "to influence." *Effect* as a noun means "a result" and, rarely, as a verb means "to cause something to happen."

Because CFCs may **affect** the ozone layer with an uncertain **effect** on global warming, our goal is to **effect** changes in public attitudes.

aggravate, irritate *Aggravate* means "to worsen"; *irritate* means "to bother."

ain't Replace *ain't* in formal writing with *am not, is not,* or *are not.* The contractions *aren't* and *isn't* are more acceptable but are still informal.

all ready, already *All ready* means "prepared"; *already* means "by that time."

Sam was **all ready,** but the team had **already** gone.

all right Always spell this as two words, not as *alright.*

all together, altogether Use *all together* to mean "everyone"; use *altogether* to mean "completely."

We were **all together** on our plan, but it was **altogether** too much to organize by Friday.

allude, elude *Allude* means "refer indirectly"; *elude* means "escape."

allusion, illusion An *allusion* is a reference to something; an *illusion* is a vision or false belief.

a lot Even when spelled correctly as two words, not as *alot*, *a lot* may be too informal for some writing. Use *many* or *much* instead.

a.m., p.m. These abbreviations may be capitals or lowercase (see 36a).

among, between Use *between* when something involves two things; use *among* for three or more.

The fight **between** the two players led to a debate **among** the umpire and the managers.

amount, number *Amount* refers to a quantity of something that can't be divided into separate units; *number* refers to countable objects.

The recipe uses a **number** of spices and a small **amount** of milk.

an (See **a, an.**)

analytical synthesis (See **synthesis.**)

and etc. (See **etc.**)

and/or Because *and/or* is imprecise, choose one of the words, or revise.

ante-, anti- The prefix *ante-* means "before" or "predating," while *anti-* means "against" or "opposed."

antecedent The noun or pronoun to which another word (usually a pronoun) refers (see Chapter 19).

anyone, any one *Anyone* is an indefinite pronoun; you may also use *any* to modify *one*, in the sense of "any individual thing or person."

Anyone can dive, but the coach has little time for **any one** person.

anyplace Replace this term in formal writing with *anywhere*, or revise.

anyways, anywheres Avoid these versions of *anyway* and *anywhere*.

appositive A noun or pronoun that renames or stands for a prior noun.

appositive phrase An **appositive** (usually a noun) and its modifiers that rename or stand for a prior noun to add detail to a sentence.

Ken and Beth, **my classmates,** won an award.

as, like Used as a preposition, *as* indicates a precise comparison. *Like* indicates a resemblance or similarity.

Remembered **as** a man of habit, Kant, **like** many other philosophers, was thoughtful and intense.

as to *As to* is considered informal in many contexts.

INFORMAL	The media speculated **as to** the film's success.
EDITED	The media speculated **about** the film's success.

assure, ensure, insure Use *assure* to imply a promise, *ensure* to imply a certain outcome, and *insure* to imply something legal or financial.

The surgeon **assured** the pianist that his hands would heal by May. To **ensure** that, the musician **insured** his hands with Lloyd's of London.

at In writing, drop *at* in direct and indirect questions.

SPOKEN	Jones asked where his attorney was **at.**
EDITED	Jones asked where his attorney **was.**

awful, awfully Use *awful* (adjective) to modify a noun; use *awfully* (adverb) to modify a verb.

He played **awfully** on that hole and sent an **awful** shot into the pond.

awhile, a while *Awhile* (one word) acts as an adverb; it is not preceded by a preposition. *A while* acts as a noun (with the article *a*) and is used in prepositional phrases.

The homeless family stayed **awhile** at the shelter because the children had not eaten for **a while.**

bad, badly Use *bad* (adjective) with a noun or linking verb expressing feelings, not the adverb *badly* (see 21f).

because, since Use *since* to indicate time, not causality in place of the more formal and precise *because*.

being as, being that Write *because* instead.

beside, besides Use *beside* to mean "next to." Use *besides* for "also" (adverb) or "except" (adjective).

Besides being the firm's tax specialist, Klein would review nearly any document placed **beside** him.

better, had better Revise to *ought to* or *should* in formal writing.

between (See **among, between.**)

block quotation A quotation long enough to require separating it from the text in an indented block (see 12b).

bring, take *Bring* implies movement from somewhere else to close at hand; *take* implies the opposite direction.

> **Bring** more coffee, but **take** away the muffins.

broke *Broke* is the past tense of *break*, not the past participle (see 21a).

| DRAFT | The computer was **broke.** |
| EDITED | The computer was **broken.** |

burst, bursted *Burst* implies an outward explosion: The boys *burst* the balloon. Do not use *bursted* for the past tense.

bust, busted Avoid *bust* or *busted* to mean "broke."

| COLLOQUIAL | The van **bust** down on the trip. |
| EDITED | The van **broke** down on the trip. |

but however, but yet Choose one word of each pair.

can, may *Can* implies ability; *may* implies permission or uncertainty.

> Bart **can** drive, but his dad **may** not lend him the car.

can't hardly, can't scarcely Use these positively (*can hardly, can scarcely*), or simply use *can't* (see 21f).

capital, capitol *Capital* refers to a government center, a letter, or money; *capitol* refers to a government building.

censor, censure *Censor* means the act of shielding something from the public, such as a book. *Censure* implies punishment or critical labeling.

center around Use *center on, focus on,* or *revolve around.*

choose, chose Use *choose* for the present and *chose* for the past tense.

cite, site *Cite* means to acknowledge someone's work; *site* means a place.

> Phil **cited** field studies of the Anasazi **site.**

clause A word group with a subject and a verb. A **main** (independent) clause can stand on its own; a **subordinate** (dependent) clause begins with a subordinating word (*because*, *although*, *which*, *that*) and cannot stand alone (see 27b).

Because he lost his balance, Sam fell on the ice.

climactic, climatic *Climactic* refers to the culmination of something; *climatic* refers to weather conditions.

comma splice Two or more sentences (main clauses) incorrectly joined with a comma. (See Chapter 18.)

comparative The form of an adjective or adverb showing that the word it modifies is compared to one other thing (see 21g and p. 231). The comparative form adds *-er* or *more* (*faster, more adept*). (See **superlative.**)

compare to, compare with Use *compare to* and *liken to* for similarities between two things. Use *compare with* for both similarities and differences.

Compared with the boy's last illness, this virus, which the doctor **compared to** a tiny army, was mild.

complement A word (noun, pronoun, adjective) or phrase tied to a subject by a **linking verb** (*becomes, is, seems*). A **subject complement** describes or renames a subject: Nan seems **tired**. An **object complement** does the same for a direct object: Brad ate the pizza **cold**. (See p. 225).

complement, compliment *Complement* means "an accompaniment"; *compliment* means "words of praise."

The guests **complimented** the chef on the menu, which **complemented** the event perfectly.

compound modifier Two or more words that work as a single modifier (**wood-burning** fireplace).

compound object Two or more objects joined by *and* or *both . . . and.*

compound subject Two or more subjects joined by *and* or *both . . . and.*

compound word A word made up of two or more independent words (such as *superman* or *father-in-law*).

conjunction A word that joins two elements in a sentence. **Coordinating conjunctions** (*and, but, or, nor, for, yet, so*) link grammatically equal elements—compound subjects, verbs, objects, and modifiers. **Subordinating conjunctions** (*because, although, while, if*) create a subordinate clause. (See Chapter 27.)

conjunctive adverb An adverb (*however, moreover, therefore*) that joins sentences or sentence elements, showing how they are related (see 27a).

continual, continuous *Continual* implies that something recurs; *continuous* implies that it is constant or unceasing.

> The **continual** noise of the jets was less annoying than the traffic **continuously** circling the airport.

coordinate adjectives Two adjectives, each modifying a noun on its own, separated by a comma. If the first modifies the second (which modifies the noun), they are **noncoordinate adjectives,** not separated by a comma.

coordinating conjunction One of seven words (*and, but, or, nor, for, yet, so*) that link equal elements (see 27a). (See **conjunction.**)

coordination A sentence structure using **coordinating conjunctions** to link and weight main clauses equally (see 27a, c).

could of, would of Replace these, often pronounced as they are misspelled, with *could have* or *would have.*

couple, couple of In formal writing, use *a few* or *two.*

criteria *Criteria* is the plural form of *criterion.*

> **PLURAL**   The **criteria** <u>were</u> too strict to follow.

critical synthesis (See **synthesis.**)

curriculum *Curriculum* is the singular form. For the plural, use either *curricula* or *curriculums* consistently.

dangling modifier (See **misplaced modifier.**)

data Widely used for both singular and plural, *data* technically is plural; *datum* refers to a single piece of data. If in doubt, use the plural.

> **PLURAL**   These **data** <u>are</u> not very revealing.

different from, different than Use *different from* when an object follows; use *different than* (not *from what*) when a clause follows.

> Jim's tacos are **different from** Lena's; his enchiladas now are **different than** they were when he began to cook.

direct quotation A statement that repeats someone's exact words, set off by quotation marks (see 33b). (See also **indirect quotation.**)

discreet, discrete *Discreet* means "reserved or cautious"; *discrete* means "distinctive" or "explicit."

disinterested, uninterested *Disinterested* implies impartiality or objectivity; *uninterested* implies lack of interest.

disruptive modifier (See **misplaced modifier.**)

done *Done* is a past participle, not past tense (see 21a).

| DRAFT | The runner **done** her best at the meet. |
| EDITED | The runner **did** her best at the meet. |

don't, doesn't Contractions may be too informal in some contexts. Ask your reader, or err on the side of formality (*do not, does not*).

double negative Avoid double negatives (see 21f).

DRAFT	The state **hasn't** done **nothing** about it.
EDITED	The state **has** done **nothing** about it.
EDITED	The state **hasn't** done **anything** about it.

due to To mean "because," use *due to* only after a form of the verb *be*. Avoid the wordy *due to the fact that.*

DRAFT	The mayor collapsed **due to** fatigue.
EDITED	The mayor's collapse was **due to** fatigue.
EDITED	The mayor collapsed **because** of fatigue.

effect, affect (See **affect, effect.**)

e.g. Avoid this abbreviation meaning "for example."

| AWKWARD | Her positions on issues, **e.g.,** gun control, are very liberal. |
| EDITED | Her positions on issues **such as** gun control are very liberal. |

ellipsis A series of three spaced periods showing a reader where something has been left out of a quotation (see 40d).

emigrate from, immigrate to People *emigrate from* one country and *immigrate to* another. *Migrate* implies moving about (*migrant workers*) or settling temporarily.

ensure (See **assure, ensure, insure.**)

enthused Avoid *enthused* for *enthusiastic* in writing.

especially, specially *Especially* implies "in particular"; *specially* means "for a specific purpose."

It was **especially** important to follow the **specially** designed workouts.

etc. Avoid this abbreviation in formal writing; supply a complete list, or use a phrase like *so forth*.

| INFORMAL | The march was a disaster: it rained, the protesters had no food, **etc.** |
| EDITED | The march was a disaster: the protesters were wet and hungry. |

eventually, ultimately Use *eventually* to imply that an outcome follows a series (or lapse) of events; use *ultimately* to imply that a final act ends a series of events.

Eventually, the rescuers pulled the last victim from the wreck, and **ultimately** there were no casualties.

everyday, every day *Everyday* (adjective) modifies a noun. *Every day* is a noun (*day*) modified by *every*.

Every day in the Peace Corps, Monique faced the **everyday** task of boiling her drinking water.

everyone, every one *Everyone* is a pronoun; *every one* is an adjective followed by a noun.

Everyone was dazzled by **every one** of the desserts.

exam In formal writing, readers may prefer the full term, *examination*.

except (See **accept, except**.)

expletive construction Opening with *there is*, *there are*, or *it is* to delay the subject until later in the sentence (see 22b).

explicit, implicit *Explicit* means that something is openly stated, *implicit* that it is implied or suggested.

farther, further *Farther* implies a distance that can be measured; *further* implies one that cannot.

The **farther** they hiked, the **further** their friendship deteriorated.

faulty parallelism (See **parallelism.**)

faulty predication A sentence flaw in which the second part (the predicate) comments on a topic different from the one in the first part (see 23a–b).

> **FAULTY**   The **presence** of ozone in smog is the **chemical** that causes eye irritation.

> **EDITED**   The **ozone** in smog is the **chemical** that causes eye irritation.

female, male Use these terms only to call attention to gender specifically, as in a research report. Otherwise, use *man* or *woman* unless such usage is sexist (see 29b).

fewer, less Use *fewer* for things that can be counted, and use *less* for quantities that cannot be divided.

> The new bill had **fewer** supporters and **less** media coverage.

first person Pronouns (*I*, *we*) for the person speaking. (See **person.**)

firstly Use *first*, *second*, *third* when enumerating points.

form The spelling or ending that shows a word's role in a sentence. (See Chapter 21.)

former, latter *Former* means "the one before" and *latter* means "the one after." The pair must refer to only two things.

fragment Part of a sentence incorrectly treated as complete. (See 17a–b.)

freshman, freshmen Readers may consider these terms sexist. Unless you are using an established term (such as the Freshman Colloquium), use *first-year student*.

fused sentence Two or more complete sentences incorrectly joined without any punctuation; also called a **run-on sentence.** (See Chapter 18.)

genre The form or type of text to which a work conforms (play, novel, lab report, essay, memo).

get Replace this word with more specific verbs.

> **INFORMAL**   King's last speeches **got** nostalgic.

> **EDITED**   King's last speeches **turned** nostalgic.

go, say Some speakers use *go* and *goes* very informally for *say* and *says*. Revise this usage in all writing.

gone, went Do not use *went* (the past tense of *go*) in place of the past participle form *gone*.

DRAFT   The officers **should have went** to the captain.

EDITED   The officers **should have gone** to the captain.

good and In formal writing, avoid this term to mean "very" (*good and* tired).

good, well *Good* (an adjective) means "favorable" (a *good* trip). *Well* (an adverb) means "done favorably." Avoid informal uses of *good* for *well*.

got to Avoid *got* or *got to* in place of *must* or *have to*.

SPOKEN   I **got to** improve my grade in statistics.

WRITTEN   I **have to** improve my grade in statistics.

great Formally, avoid *great* as an adjective meaning "wonderful"; use it to mean "large" or "monumental."

hanged, hung Some readers will expect you to use *hanged* exclusively to mean execution by hanging and *hung* to refer to anything else.

have, got (See **got to.**)

have, of (See **could of, would of.**)

he, she Avoid privileging male forms (see 29b).

helping verb A form of a verb such as *be*, *do*, or *have* that can be combined with a main verb (see 21a).

hopefully Some readers may object when this word modifies an entire clause ("*Hopefully, her health will improve*"). When in doubt, use it only as "feeling hopeful."

however (See **but however, but yet.**)

hung (See **hanged, hung.**)

if, whether Use *if* before a specific outcome (stated or implied); use *whether* to consider alternatives.

If the technology can be perfected, we may soon have three-dimensional television. But **whether** we will be able to afford it is another question.

illogical comparison (See **incomplete sentence.**)

illusion (See **allusion, illusion.**)

immigrate to (See **emigrate from, immigrate to.**)

implicit (See **explicit, implicit.**)

incomplete comparison (See **incomplete sentence.**)

incomplete sentence A sentence that fails to complete an expected logical or grammatical pattern. An **incomplete comparison** leaves out the element to which something is compared; an **illogical comparison** seems to compare things that cannot be reasonably compared. (See Chapter 23.)

independent clause (See **main clause.**)

indirect question A sentence whose main clause is a statement and whose embedded clause asks a question. Treat these as statements, not questions.

> Phil wondered **what the study would show.**

indirect quotation A quotation in which a writer reports the substance of someone's words but not the exact words used. Quotation marks are not needed. (See **direct quotation;** see Chapter 33.)

in regard to Replace this wordy phrase with *about.*

inside of, outside of When you use *inside* or *outside* to mark locations, omit *of: Inside* the hut was a child.

insure (See **assure, ensure, insure.**)

interpolation Your own words, marked with brackets, introduced into a direct quotation from someone else (see 40c).

interrupter A parenthetical remark such as *in fact* or *more importantly.*

irregardless Avoid this erroneous form of *regardless.*

irritate (See **aggravate, irritate.**)

its, it's *Its* is a possessive pronoun; *it's* is a contraction for *it is.* (See Chapter 32.) Some readers object to contractions in formal writing.

-ize, -wise Some readers object to turning nouns or adjectives into verbs by adding *-ize* (*finalize, itemize, computerize*). Avoid adding *-wise* to words: "Weather-*wise*, it's chilly."

keyword A word in a database, catalog, or index used to identify a topic.

kind, sort, type Precede these singular nouns with *this,* not *these.* In general, use more precise words.

kind of, sort of Avoid these informal expressions (meaning "a little," "rather," or "somewhat") in academic and workplace writing.

latter (See **former, latter.**)

lay, lie *Lay* is a verb that needs a direct object (not the self). *Lie*, "place in a resting position," refers to the self; it takes the past tense form *lay* (see pp. 152–153).

less (See **fewer, less.**)

lie (See **lay, lie.**)

like (See **as, like.**)

limiting modifier A word such as *only*, *almost*, or *just* that qualifies a word, usually the one that follows it. (See 24a.)

linking verb A verb that expresses a state of being or an occurrence: *is*, *seems*, *becomes*, *grows*.

literally In both factual and figurative (not true to fact) statements, avoid *literally*.

DRAFT	Jed **literally** died when he saw the hotel.
REDUNDANT	Jed **literally gasped** when he saw the hotel.
EDITED	Jed **gasped** when he saw the hotel.

loose, lose *Loose* (rhyming with *moose*) is an adjective meaning "not tight." *Lose* (rhyming with *snooze*) is a present tense verb meaning "to misplace."

lots (See **a lot.**)

main clause A word group with a subject and a verb that can stand on its own as a sentence. (See **clause.**)

may (See **can, may.**)

maybe, may be *Maybe* means *possibly; may be* is part of a verb structure.

The President **may be** speaking now, so **maybe** we should listen.

media, medium Technically plural, *media* is frequently used as a singular noun to refer to the press. *Medium* generally refers to a conduit or method of transmission.

The **media** is not covering the story accurately.

The telephone is a useful **medium** for planning.

might of (See **could of, would of.**)

mighty In formal writing, omit or replace *mighty* with *very*.

misplaced modifier A modifier incorrectly placed relative to the word it modifies (its headword). (See Chapter 24.)

mixed sentence A sentence with a mismatched or shifted grammatical structure. (See Chapter 23.)

modifier A word or word group, acting as an adjective or adverb, that qualifies the meaning of another word (see 21e–f).

modify The function of adjectives and adverbs that add to, qualify, limit, or extend the meaning of other words.

Ms. To avoid sexist labeling of women by marital status (not marked in men's titles), use *Ms.* unless you have reason to use *Miss* or *Mrs.* (as in the name of the character *Mrs. Dalloway*). Use professional titles when appropriate (*Dr.*, *Professor*, *Senator*, *Mayor*).

must of, must have (See **could of, would of.**)

nominalization A noun (*modernization*, *verbosity*) created from a verb (*modernize*) or adjective (*verbose*). (See 22b.)

noncoordinate adjectives (See **coordinate adjectives.**)

nonrestrictive modifier (See **restrictive modifier.**)

nor, or Use *nor* for negative and *or* for positive constructions.

NEGATIVE	Neither rain **nor** snow will slow the team.
POSITIVE	Either rain **or** snow may delay the game.

nothing like, nowhere near In formal writing, avoid these informal phrases used to compare two things.

noun string A sequence of nouns used to modify a main noun (*multifunction modulation control device*) that may seem abstract or technical to readers.

nowheres Use *nowhere* instead.

number The way of showing whether a noun or pronoun is **singular** (one) or **plural** (two or more). Subjects and verbs must agree in number as must pronouns and the nouns they modify. (See Chapter 20 and 25a–b; see also **amount, number.**)

object The words in a sentence that tell who or what receives the action.

The class cleaned up **the park.**

of, have (See **could of, would of.**)

off of Use *off* instead.

OK When you write formally, use *OK* only in dialogue. If you mean "good" or "acceptable," use these terms.

on account of In formal writing, use *because*.

outside of (See **inside of, outside of.**)

parallelism The expression of similar or related ideas in similar grammatical form (see Chapter 26).

paraphrase To rewrite a passage in your own words, preserving the essence and detail of the original.

passive voice (See **voice.**)

per Use *per* to mean "by the," as in *per hour*, not "according to," as in *per your instructions*.

percent, percentage Use *percent* with numbers (*10 percent*); use *percentage* for a statistical part of something (*a large percentage of the budget*).

person The form that a noun or pronoun takes to identify the subject of a sentence. **First person** is someone speaking (*I, we*); **second person** is someone spoken to (*you*); **third person** is someone being spoken about (*he, she, it, they*). (See Chapter 20 and 25a–b.)

personal pronoun A pronoun that designates persons or things, such as *I, me, you, him, we, you, they*. (See 21c–d and pp. 230–231.)

phrase A word group without a subject, a verb, or both. (See **clause.**)

plagiarism The unethical or illegal practice of using another writer's words or text as your own without acknowledging their source (see 12d).

plus Replace *plus* with *and* to join two main clauses. Use *plus* only to mean "in addition to."

possessive A pronoun (*mine, hers, yours, theirs*) or noun (*the **bird's** egg*) that expresses ownership. (See 21c and 32a–b.)

precede, proceed *Precede* means "come before"; *proceed* means "go ahead."

predicate The words in a sentence that indicate an action, relationship, or condition—typically a **verb phrase** following the subject of the sentence. A **simple predicate** is a verb or verb phrase; to these, a **complete predicate** adds modifiers or other words that receive action or complete the verb.

prefix An addition, such as *un-* in *unforgiving*, at the beginning of a word. (See **suffix.**)

pretty Use *pretty* to mean "attractive," not "somewhat" or "rather" (as in *pretty good, pretty hungry*).

primary source Research material in or close to original form (see 8e).

principal, principle *Principal* is a noun meaning "an authority" or "head of a school" or an adjective meaning "leading" ("a *principal* objection to the testimony"). *Principle* is a noun meaning "belief or conviction."

proceed (See **precede, proceed.**)

quote, quotation Formally, *quote* is a verb, and *quotation* is a noun. Some readers object to *quote* as an abbreviation of *quotation*.

raise, rise *Raise* is a transitive verb meaning "to lift up." *Rise* is an intransitive verb (it takes no object) meaning "to get up or move up."

He **raised** his head to watch the sun **rise.**

rarely ever Use *rarely* alone, not paired with *ever*.
real, really Use *real* as an adjective; use *really* as an adverb (see 21f).
reason is because, reason is that Avoid these wordy phrases (See 23b).
redundancy The use of unnecessary or repeated words (see 28a).
reference chain A sequence of pronouns whose **antecedent,** the word to which they refer, is stated in the opening sentence of a passage (see 19b).
regarding (See **in regard to.**)
regardless (See **irregardless.**)
relative clause A clause that modifies a noun or pronoun and begins with a **relative pronoun** (*who, whom, whose, which, that*).

Jen found a Web site **that** had valuable links.

respectfully, respectively Use *respectfully* for "with respect" and *respectively* to imply an order or sequence.

The senate **respectfully** submitted revisions for items 4 and 10, **respectively.**

restrictive modifier A **restrictive modifier** supplies information essential to the meaning of a sentence and is added without commas. A **nonrestrictive modifier** adds useful or interesting information not essential to the meaning and set off by commas (see 30d).
rise (See **raise, rise.**)
run-on sentence (See **fused sentence.**)

says (See **go, say.**)
second person The pronoun (*you*) referring to the person spoken to. (See **person.**)

secondary source Research information that analyzes, interprets, or comments on primary sources (see 8e). (See also **primary source.**)

sentence A group of words with both a subject and a complete verb that can stand on its own. (See **comma splice, fragment, fused sentence;** see p. 224, 17a, and Chapter 18.)

sentence cluster A group of sentences that develop related ideas or information.

set, sit *Set* means "to place"; *sit* means "to place oneself" (see pp. 152–153).

should of (See **could of, would of.**)

shift An inappropriate switch in **person, number, tense,** or topic. (See Chapter 25.)

since (See **because, since.**)

sit (See **set, sit.**)

site (See **cite, site.**)

so Some readers object to the use of *so* in place of *very*.

somebody, some body (See **anyone, any one.**)

someone, some one (See **anyone, any one.**)

sometime, some time, sometimes *Sometime* refers to a vague future time; *sometimes* means "every once in a while." *Some time* is an adjective (*some*) modifying a noun (*time*).

> **Sometime** every winter, **sometimes** after a project is finished, the crew takes **some time** off.

sort (See **kind, sort.**)

specially (See **especially, specially.**)

split infinitive An infinitive is the base form of a verb paired with *to* (*to run*). Some readers object to another word placed between the two (to **quickly** run). (See 24a.)

squinting modifier (See **misplaced modifier.**)

stationary, stationery *Stationary* means "standing still"; *stationery* refers to writing paper.

subject In a sentence, the doer or thing talked about, typically placed before a verb phrase. A **simple subject** consists of one or more nouns (or pronouns) naming the doer; to this a **complete subject** adds modifiers.

subject complement (See **complement.**)

subordinate clause A word group with a subject and a verb that is introduced by a subordinator (*because, although, that, which*). It must be connected to a main clause (which can stand alone). (See **clause;** see 27b–c.)

subordinating conjunction A word (*because*, *although*, *while*, *if*) that introduces a subordinate clause, a word group with a subject and verb that cannot stand alone and must be connected to a main clause. (See **conjunction;** see 27b.)

such Some readers will expect *that* to follow *such.*

The team solved **such** a complex problem **that** everyone cheered.

suffix An addition, such as *-ly* in *quickly*, at the end of a word. (See **prefix.**)

summary A concise restatement in your own words, boiling a passage or source down to essentials (see 11a).

superlative The form of an adjective or adverb showing that the word it modifies is compared to two or more other things (see 21g and p. 231). The superlative adds *-est* or *most* (*fastest*, *most adept*). (See **comparative.**)

suppose to Use the correct form, *supposed to*, even though the *-d* is not always heard in pronunciation. (See p. 150.)

sure, surely Formally, use *sure* to mean "certain." Use *surely*, not *sure* as an adverb (see 21f).

He has **surely** studied hard and is **sure** to pass.

sure and, try and Write *sure to* and *try to* instead.

synthesis The distilling of separate elements into a single, unified entity. For a research paper, an analytical synthesis relates summaries of several sources while a critical synthesis presents conclusions about a variety of perspectives, opinions, or interpretations (see 11b).

take (See **bring, take.**)

tense The form a verb takes to indicate time   past, present, or future tense (see 21a–b and pp. 226–228).

than, then *Than* is used to compare; *then* implies a sequence of events or a causal relationship.

Lil played harder **than** Eva; **then** the rain began.

that, which In formal writing, use *that* when a clause is essential to the meaning of a sentence (restrictive modifier) and *which* when it does not provide essential information (nonrestrictive modifier) (see 30d).

theirself, theirselves, themself Replace these with *themselves* to refer to more than one person and *himself* or *herself* to refer to one person.

them Avoid *them* as a subject or to modify a subject, as in "*Them* are fresh" or "*Them* apples are crisp." Replace with *they*, *these*, *those*, or *the* with a noun (*the apples*).

then (See **than, then.**)

there, their, they're These forms sound alike, but *there* shows location, *their* is a possessive pronoun, and *they're* contracts *they* and *are*.

Look over **there. Their** car ran out of gas. **They're** starting to walk.

third person Pronouns (*he*, *she*, *it*, *they*) that indicate the person or thing spoken about. (See **person;** see 25a–b.)

thusly Replace this term with *thus* or *therefore*.

till, until, 'til Some readers will find *'til* and *till* informal; use *until*.

to, too, two These words sound alike, but *to* is a preposition showing direction, *too* means "also," and *two* is a number.

Ed went **to** the lake **two** times and took Han **too.**

toward, towards Prefer *toward* in formal writing.

transitional expression Expressions (*therefore*, *in addition*) that link one idea, sentence, or paragraph to the next, helping readers relate ideas.

try and, try to (See **sure and, try and.**)

ultimately (See **eventually, ultimately.**)

uninterested (See **disinterested, uninterested.**)

unique Use *unique*, not *most* or *more unique* (see 21g).

until (See **till, until, 'til.**)

use to, used to Write *used to*, even though the -*d* is not always clearly pronounced. (See p. 150.)

verb The word in a sentence that expresses action (*jump*), occurrence (*happen*), or state of being (*be*). (See 21a and pp. 226–228.)

voice A verb is in the **active voice** when the doer of the action is the subject of the sentence and in the **passive voice** when the goal or object of the sentence is the subject. (See p. 164 and p. 228.)

wait for, wait on Use *wait on* for a clerk's or server's job; use *wait for* to mean "to await someone's arrival."

well (See **good, well.**)

went (See **gone, went.**)

were, we're *Were* is a verb; *we're* is a contraction for "we are."

where . . . at (See **at**.)

whether (See **if, whether**.)

which (See **that, which**.)

who, whom Though the distinction between these words is disappearing, many readers will expect you to use *whom* for an object. Err on the side of formality, or rewrite (see p. 155).

who's, whose *Who's* is a contraction for "who is"; *whose* shows possession.

-wise (See **-ize, -wise**.)

would of (See **could of, would of**.)

yet (See **but however, but yet**.)

your, you're *Your* is a possessive pronoun; *you're* contracts "you are."

If **you're** taking math, you'll need **your** calculator.

Credits *(continued from p. vi)*

http://digestive.niddk.nih.gov/ddiseases/pubs/lactoseintolerance/index.htm. Reprinted with permission. **Page 56:** Donald Hall, "A Small Fig Tree," from OLD AND NEW POEMS. Copyright © 1990 by Donald Hall. Reprinted by permission of Ticknor Fields/Houghton Mifflin Co. All rights reserved. **Page 57–58:** Laurie Garrett, THE COMING PLAGUE (New York: Penguin Books, 1994). **Page 61:** From MLA HANDBOOK FOR WRITERS OF RESEARCH PAPERS by Joseph Gibaldi. Published by Modern Language Association. Copyright © 2003 Modern Language Association. Reprinted by permission of the Modern Language Association. **Page 61:** From PUBLICATION MANUAL OF THE AMERICAN PSYCHOLOGICAL ASSOCIATION, 5th edition, page xxiii, which was published by the American Psychological Association. Copyright © 2001 by The American Psychological Association. Reprinted by permission. **Page 65:** Michael Bright, ANIMAL LANGUAGE (Ithaca, NY: Cornell University Press, 1984). **Page 65:** Maureen Honey, CREATING ROSIE THE RIVETER (University of Massachusetts Press, 1984). **Page 66:** Committee of Concerned Journalists, "A Statement of Concern," THE MEDIA AND MORALITY, edited by Robert M. Baird, William E. Loges, and Stuart E. Rosenbaum (New York: Prometheus Books, 1999). **Page 67:** Mark Twain, HUCKLEBERRY FINN (New York: HarperCollins, 1987). **Page 69:** Wayland D. Hand, "Folk Medical Magic and Symbolism in the West," in MAGIC, WITCHCRAFT AND RELIGION: An Anthropological Study of the Supernatural, 3rd edition, Arthur C. Lehmann and James E. Myers, eds. (Mayfield Publishing, 1993). **Page 69:** George Gmelch, "Baseball Magic." TRANSACTION, 1971. **Page 72:** Juliet B. Schor, THE OVERWORKED AMERICAN (New York: HarperCollins, 1998). **Page 94:** Avi Sadeh, Amiram Raviv, and Reut Gruber, "Sleep Patterns and Sleep Disruptions in School-Age Children," DEVELOPMENTAL PSYCHOLOGY, Vol. 36, No. 3, May 2000. **Page 116:** John Edgar Wideman, BROTHERS AND KEEPERS (New York: Random House, 1984). **Page 128:** Claude F. Boutron et al., "Decrease in Anthropologic Lead, Cadmium, and Zinc in Greenland Snows since the Late 1960's," NATURE, Vol. 353, 1991. **Page 133:** Joan Didion, "Why I Write." From THE NEW YORK TIMES MAGAZINE,

(Credits continue on p. 264)

Index

Guide to ESL Advice

Look for the ESL Advice if your first language is not English. This advice is integrated throughout the handbook and highlighted so it's easy to spot.

On Agreement

Separated Subjects and Verbs (**20b**)
Quantifiers (**20b**)
This, That, These, Those (**20c**)

On Articles and Nouns

Articles and Nouns (**21f**)

On Sentences

Similar Connecting Words (**18c**)
There and *It* as Subjects (**22b**)
Structures for Coordination and Subordination (**27c**)

On Verbs

Common Helping Verbs (**21a**)
Conditional Statements (**21a**)
Verb Tense and Expressions of Time (**25c**)

On Prepositions

Prepositions (**p. 232**)

On Punctuation and Mechanics

Quotation Marks (**33a**)
Abbreviated Titles (**36a**)

Credits (*continued from p. 251*)

December 5, 1976. Copyright 1976 by Joan Didion and The New York Times Company. **Page 161:** Mark Twain, from a letter to George Bainton, October 1888. **Page 185:** Frank L. Visco, from HOW TO WRITE GOOD. **Page 199:** Frank Goddio, "San Diego: An Account of Adventure, Deceit, and Intrigue," NATIONAL GEOGRAPHIC, 1994. **Page 204:** Robert Daseler, LEVERING AVENUE POEMS (Evansville: The University of Evansville Press, 1998). **Page 220:** Sir Philip Sidney, "His Lady's Cruelty," THE OXFORD BOOK OF ENGLISH VERSE 1250–1918 (London: Oxford University Press, 1973). Student Acknowledgments: Summer Arrigo-Nelson, Kimlee Cunningham, Jennifer Figliozzi, Daisy Garcia, Tammy Jo Helton, Jenny Latimer, Sharon Salamone.

Boldface numbers refer to sections and chapters in the handbook.

abbrev	incorrect abbreviation, 36		p, punc	punctuation error, 30–33, 38
add	information needed, 4c		⌃	comma, 30
agr	error in agreement, 20		no ⌃	no comma, 30
apos	apostrophe error, 32		; :	semicolon, colon, 31
art	incorrect article, 21f		⌄	apostrophe, 32
awk	awkward construction, 22		" "	quotation marks, 12b, 33
cap	capital letter needed, 35		. ? !	end marks, 40f
case	incorrect pronoun form, 21c–d		( ) [ ]	parentheses, brackets,
clear	clearer sentence needed, 22		— ... /	dashes, ellipses, slashes, 40
coh	coherence needed, 4b		prep	preposition error, p. 232
coord	faulty coordination, 27a, 27c		pr ref	pronoun reference error, 19
			proof?	evidence needed, 3b–c
cs	comma splice, 18a, 18c		reorg	reorganize, 1b, 4
cut	unneeded material, 1b, 28		rep	repetitious, 28
dev	development needed, 4c		sent	sentence revision needed, 1b, 22
discrm	discriminatory, 29b		shift	shift, 25
dm	dangling modifier, 24		sp, spell	spelled incorrectly, 39
dneg	double negative, 21f		sub	faulty subordination, 27b–c
emph	emphasis needed, 22b		t, tense	wrong verb tense, 21a–b, p. 226
focus	focus needed, 4a			
frag	sentence fragment, 17		trans	transition needed, 4b
fs	fused sentence, 18b–c		und	underlining (italics), 34
gap	explanation needed, 1b, 3		us	error in usage, Glossary
hyph	hyphen (-) needed, 38		var	sentence variety needed, 22b
inc	incomplete sentence, 23			
ital	italics (underlining), 34		verb	incorrect verb form, 21a
lc	lowercase letter needed, 35		wc, ww	word choice, wrong word
link	linkage needed, 4b–c			
log	faulty reasoning, 3		wordy	too many words, 28
mixed	mixed sentence, 23		∧	insert
mm	misplaced modifier, 24		⟆	delete
modif	incorrect adjective or adverb, 21e–g		⌒	close up space
			∿	transpose letters or words
num	incorrect number, 37		#	add a space
//	parallel elements needed, 26		X	obvious error
¶	paragraph, 4			

Contents